Management from A to Z and Back Again

More business and management titles from Critical Publishing

Agile Resilience – The Psychology of Developing Resilience in the Workplace
by Tom Dillon, edited by Bob Thomson
978-1-914171-65-9

And the Leader is… – Transforming Cultures with CEQ
by Gareth Chick
978-1-912508-36-5

Corporate Emotional Intelligence – Being Human in a Corporate World
by Gareth Chick
978-1-912508-04-4

How to Thrive at Work – Mindfulness, Motivation and Productivity
by Stephen J Mordue and Lisa Watson
978-1-913453-69-5

Leading with Empathy – Supporting People in a Hybrid World
by Carolyn Reily, edited by Bob Thomson
978-1-915080-59-2

Transforming Performance at Work – The Power of Positive Psychology
by Sarah Alexander, edited by Bob Thomson
978-1-914171-83-3

To order our books please go to our website www.criticalpublishing.com or contact our distributor Ingram Publisher Services, telephone 01752 202301 or email IPSUK.orders@ingramcontent.com. Details of bulk order discounts can be found at www.criticalpublishing.com/delivery-information.

Our titles are also available in electronic format: for individual use via our website and for libraries and other institutions from all the major ebook platforms.

Management
from A to Z
and Back Again

> **52 ideas, tools and models for managing people**

BOB THOMSON

First published in 2024 by Critical Publishing Ltd

All rights reserved. No part of this publication may be reproduced, stored in a retrieval system, or transmitted in any form or by any means, electronic, mechanical, photocopying, recording or otherwise, without prior permission in writing from the publisher.

The author has made every effort to ensure the accuracy of information contained in this publication, but assumes no responsibility for any errors, inaccuracies, inconsistencies and omissions. Likewise, every effort has been made to contact copyright holders. If any copyright material has been reproduced unwittingly and without permission the Publisher will gladly receive information enabling them to rectify any error or omission in subsequent editions.

Copyright © 2024 Bob Thomson

British Library Cataloguing in Publication Data
A CIP record for this book is available from the British Library

ISBN: 978-1-915713-51-3

This book is also available in the following e-book formats:
EPUB ISBN: 978-1-915713-52-0
Adobe e-book ISBN: 978-1-915713-53-7

The right of Bob Thomson to be identified as the Author of this work has been asserted by him in accordance with the Copyright, Design and Patents Act 1988.

Text design by Greensplash
Cover design by Out of House Limited
Project management by Newgen Publishing UK

Critical Publishing
3 Connaught Road
St Albans
AL3 5RX

www.criticalpublishing.com

CONTENTS

About the author — viii
List of figures and tables — ix

Introduction — 1

FROM A TO Z — 3

Chapter 1: A	Authenticity	5
Chapter 2: B	Eric Berne and some ideas from Transactional Analysis	9
Chapter 3: C	Coaching and mentoring	14
Chapter 4: D	Delegation and micromanagement	19
Chapter 5: E	Emotional intelligence	24
Chapter 6: F	Fierce conversations	30
Chapter 7: G	Growing people	35
Chapter 8: H	Ron Heifetz and Adaptive Leadership	40
Chapter 9: I	Influencing and power	45
Chapter 10: J	Carl Jung and the Myers–Briggs Type Indicator	50
Chapter 11: K	John Kotter: leadership is different from management	55
Chapter 12: L	Leading with love	61
Chapter 13: M	Managing meetings	65
Chapter 14: N	Saying *no*: managing your time	70
Chapter 15: O	Images of organisation	75
Chapter 16: P	Performance and development reviews	81

Chapter 17: Q	Questioning and playing back	86
Chapter 18: R	Management as a relationship	91
Chapter 19: S	Servant leadership	96
Chapter 20: T	Managing a team	101
Chapter 21: U	UN Sustainable Development Goals	107
Chapter 22: V	Virtue ethics	112
Chapter 23: W	Work–life balance	116
Chapter 24: X	Theory X and Theory Y	121
Chapter 25: Y	Getting to yes	126
Chapter 26: Z	Zoom and hybrid working	131

AND BACK AGAIN 137

Chapter 27: Z	Zookeeping	139
Chapter 28: Y	Your purpose and values	145
Chapter 29: X	Generation X and Generation Y	150
Chapter 30: W	Well-being in the workplace	155
Chapter 31: V	Vision and strategy	161
Chapter 32: U	Understanding context	166
Chapter 33: T	Talent management	171
Chapter 34: S	Shadow of the leader	176
Chapter 35: R	Romance of leadership and followership	180
Chapter 36: Q	Quiet leadership	185
Chapter 37: P	Positive Psychology	190
Chapter 38: O	Organisational culture	197
Chapter 39: N	National culture	204
Chapter 40: M	Managing change	210
Chapter 41: L	Listening	217
Chapter 42: K	Creating institutional knowledge	222
Chapter 43: J	John Adair's Action-Centred Leadership model	228

Chapter 44: I	The inner game	233
Chapter 45: H	Humility	237
Chapter 46: G	Games people play	242
Chapter 47: F	Giving, generating and gathering feedback	247
Chapter 48: E	Handling emails	252
Chapter 49: D	Decision-making	256
Chapter 50: C	Confidence	262
Chapter 51: B	Business schools	267
Chapter 52: A	Assertiveness	271

| Index | | 277 |

About the author

Bob Thomson is a professor at Warwick Business School. He has many years of experience working in leadership and management development in the energy industry and in higher education. He is accredited as a coach and supervisor by the European Mentoring and Coaching Council, and is a qualified and experienced mediator. He has written eight previous books on coaching, managing people, and learning from experience. He is the editor of Critical Publishing's *Business in Mind* series of books on mental well-being in the workplace, and the author of *Coaching from A to Z and Back Again*.

List of figures and tables

Figures

2.1	Transactions	10
5.1	A framework for emotional intelligence	25
7.1	The cycle of learning from experience	35
14.1	The urgent–important matrix	71
16.1	A framework for a performance and development review	82
18.1	The managerial grid: concern for task and concern for people	92
21.1	The Pentad	110
24.1	Maslow's hierarchy of needs	123
25.1	Five ways of handling conflict	129
26.1	Work arrangements in place and time	132
27.1	A model of political behaviour	142
35.1	A model of followership	182
40.1	William Bridges' transition curve	213
41.1	The ladder of listening	218
42.1	Four types of information	224
42.2	The Coverdale systematic approach	226
46.1	The drama triangle	243
46.2	The winner's triangle	245
50.1	A cycle of development	265
52.1	Assertive, aggressive and passive stances	272

Tables

3.1	A spectrum of directive to non-directive coaching behaviours	14
3.2	The coaching dance	17

11.1	Leadership and management	55
33.1	Competency framework example	172
39.1	Data for six countries on Hofstede's dimensions of national culture	206
39.2	Meyer's eight dimensions of national culture	207
52.1	Rights and responsibilities	273

Introduction

I worked in management development in the energy sector for 17 years before joining the University of Warwick in 2005, first in an internal staff development role and then as an academic at Warwick Business School. In this book I explore models and frameworks that I have found valuable in my work in learning and development, and also with coaching clients. I set out a variety of ideas that invite you to reflect upon and enhance how you manage yourself and the people who work for you. I also share some personal reflections and experiences.

The book focuses on the human and relationship aspects of management – *soft skills*, as it were – rather than topics such as finance or strategy. Managing people is a challenge in every organisation in every part of the world. Building effective relationships with the people that you manage is the foundation for high performance and for supporting their well-being and development. Managing yourself is also a challenge, and is the basis for creating a satisfying work–life balance and for looking after your own well-being.

The 52 chapters which follow – from A to Z and back again – are all around 1000 words in length. Each chapter offers ideas for you to consider, digest or reject, and perhaps try out in practice. There is a suggested resource – a video or a written piece – at the end of each chapter to illustrate or expand upon the material. The order of the chapters was determined by the alphabet. You may choose to read each chapter in turn, or select the topics that interest you most. I enjoyed writing to this format, and I hope that you enjoy reading it too. Finally, I'd like to thank Julia Morris, Lily Harrison and their colleagues at Critical Publishing, and Clare Owen and Annie Rose of Newgen Publishing, for their practical support and guidance in the production of the book.

Bob Thomson

From A to Z

Chapter 1: A
AUTHENTICITY

One of my main responsibilities in my role at Warwick Business School is to lead a module for our full-time MBA students called LeadershipPlus. Each year we have around 120 students from all over the world on the programme. The aims of the module are to help each of the students to understand themselves more deeply, to enhance their ability to work in a team, and to develop their management and leadership skills. It is a distinctive module, highly experiential in nature, and is a valuable asset in recruiting students to the programme. Most of the students find it both enjoyable and valuable, while there are always a few who hate it and would prefer a more academic exploration of leadership.

At the opening of the module, I share two slides. The first reads:

Who you are is how you lead.

I say to the students that taking part in the module – and in the MBA overall – is a journey in which they will learn a lot about themselves. My hope is that they will take these learnings back to the world of work after they've finished their MBA. I suggest that the person you are – your values, your strengths and weaknesses, your personality, the things that motivate you, and your hopes and fears – will shape how you approach the challenge of leading and managing others. Similarly, in this book I invite you to explore how you can draw upon your authentic self as a foundation for managing other people effectively. The proposition that underlies the book is that knowing and accepting your authentic self sits at the heart of creating successful working relationships with the people that you manage.

I don't wish to appear naïve here. I realise that there are managers in many organisations that lack self-awareness or don't know – or care about – how they impact on others. And there are others who deliberately manipulate, lie or cheat in order to get people to do what they want them to do. You can use power to pursue your own ends, ignoring the stress or hurt you cause others – and some people have risen to the top of organisations largely on this basis. I have the working title of another book that would explore such an approach – it would be called *The Bastard's Guide to Management*. I can think of a few high profile politicians who would contribute the preface. But I'll never write it!

Moreover, having a clear sense of your values, your priorities, your ambitions, and your strengths and weaknesses provides a foundation for managing yourself – for pursuing your goals, developing your career, and creating the type of work–life balance that you want. I'll explore how you manage yourself in various ways in later chapters.

The second slide that I share at the start of the LeadershipPlus module reads:

How you lead depends on where you are.

Your approach to management needs to reflect the context in which you're operating. For example, managing talented, motivated people in an organisation which is well resourced is very different from managing people who don't have the necessary skills, knowledge or resources to do the job. Different organisations have different cultures and rules – managing in a young high-tech business is likely to be different from managing in a more bureaucratic setting such as a government department. Similarly, managing people in a UK culture is likely to differ in important ways from managing in a country such as China or India.

It is easier to manage authentically when you can trust the people that you're managing. I'm not suggesting that you trust everyone. Some people can't be trusted – perhaps to do a particular task that they aren't capable of or perhaps in a much wider, general sense they are untrustworthy.

Managing people is about relationships. You create a relationship with everyone that you manage. And you can't help but create a relationship. For example, it might be that you haven't spoken to one of your reports for ages – that in itself shapes the nature of the relationship.

Authentic leadership

In his book *Authentic Leadership*, Bill George writes:

> *After years of studying leaders and their traits, I believe that leadership begins and ends with authenticity. It's being yourself; being the person you were created to be.*
> (George, 2003)

He goes on to say that to be an authentic leader, you need to:

- understand your purpose – which requires understanding yourself, your passions, and your underlying motivations;
- practise solid values – these define your moral compass;
- lead with heart – being open, willing to share yourself, and genuinely interested in others;
- establish connected relationships – open, deep relationships that build trust and commitment;
- demonstrate self-discipline – which translates your values into consistent actions.

In a Harvard Business School blog Matt Gavin (2019) offers this definition of *authentic leadership*:

> *Authentic leadership is a leadership style exhibited by individuals who have high standards of integrity, take responsibility for their actions, and make decisions based*

on principle rather than short-term success. They use their inner compasses to guide their daily actions, which enables them to earn the trust of their employees, peers, and shareholders – creating approachable work environments and boosting team performance.

Authentic leadership's key differentiator is the motivation behind it. An authentic leader strives to create a meaningful relationship with their team as they work toward goals related to their organization's mission and purpose – not just its bottom line.

One of the points made by both Bill George and Matt Gavin is that authentic leadership looks beyond short-term financial results. Authentic leaders have a sense of mission which they commit to, and which they enable others to believe in and identify with.

> **VIDEO**
>
> Good Leader Are Authentic Leader – Bill George (APB Speakers, 2016): www.youtube.com/watch?v=kubBp9A3BDE
>
> In this five-minute video Bill George shares a personal experience of rediscovering his authenticity as a person and as a leader.

References

Gavin, M (2019) Authentic Leadership: What it Is and Why it's Important. Harvard Business School Online, 10 December. [online] Available at: https://online.hbs.edu/blog/post/authentic-leadership (accessed 27 February 2024).

George, B (2003) *Authentic Leadership*. San Francisco: Jossey-Bass.

Chapter 2: B
ERIC BERNE AND SOME IDEAS FROM TRANSACTIONAL ANALYSIS

Eric Berne was a Canadian-born psychiatrist who created the theory of Transactional Analysis (TA) as a way of explaining human behaviour. TA is a psychological theory that seeks to explain how individuals think, feel, behave and interact with others, often in patterns that are repeated through life. It is a way of understanding what happens within and between people. TA is fundamentally a psychoanalytic approach which assumes that our early childhood experiences profoundly shape – generally unconsciously – how we live our lives.

In 1964 Berne published a bestselling book, *Games People Play*. Although criticised in academic circles as lacking research or scientific support, TA expresses its key ideas in clear and often memorable language. For example, the title of another bestselling book on TA is *I'm OK, You're OK* by Thomas Harris (1969).

Ego states and transactions

A fundamental notion in TA is the idea of Parent, Adult and Child ego states. (TA uses initial capital letters for ego states.) At any moment in time, each of us is in a particular emotional and psychological state, known in TA as an *ego state*. When we are in a *Parent* ego state, we are thinking, feeling and behaving in ways that reflect how our parents, or other authority figures such as older siblings or teachers, acted towards us in our early childhood years. The Parent ego states splits in two. We may be in

Critical Parent, reflecting in some way how we experienced discipline, criticism or lack of affection, or in *Nurturing Parent*, seeking to look after others. Similarly, we might be in an *Adapted Child* ego state, replaying attitudes and behaviours that we learnt and displayed in order to comply with the disciplinary demands of others, or in *Free Child*, where we are playful, lively and imaginative – as we sometimes were when we were kids. In our *Adult* ego state (which does not split in two), we are present in the here and now, aware of what's happening to ourself and others, and focused on the current issue or challenge.

TA is concerned with the communications or transactions between people and the relationships thereby created. When someone says something and the other person responds, this is termed a transaction. Transactions – a stimulus plus a response – are the building blocks of communication. Figure 2.1 shows two patterns of interaction: – a Parent–Child transaction and an Adult–Adult transaction.

Figure 2.1 Transactions

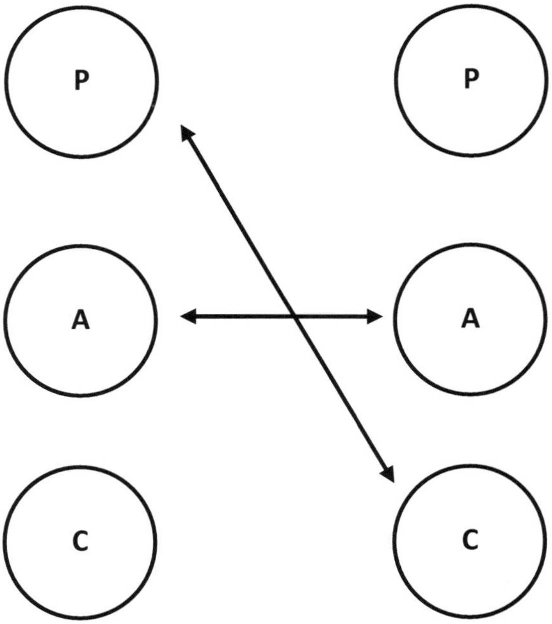

In thinking about transactions, or more generally relationships, in a work context, a common pattern of interaction is that a manager operates from a Critical Parent ego state, which prompts an Adapted Child response from someone who reports to them. Indeed, the whole culture of a department or an organisation might be characterised by such Parent–Child interactions between managers and reports. This is likely to be an environment of command and control.

There can be a number of problems with such a Parent–Child relationship between a manager and one (or all) of their team. The bulk of the responsibility for action and results sits heavily with the manager, increasing the demands and pressures on their time. The person who reports to them is less likely to feel accountable, to use their initiative and to offer their ideas. Hence, they will grow and develop less in their role.

In contrast, a manager who seeks to create an Adult–Adult way of operating with the members of their team will be willing to delegate more, freeing themselves up to, for example, think strategically or to have a better work–life balance. Team members take responsibility, make a greater contribution and feel more motivated. When this becomes the norm, over time their sense of self, their competence and their confidence develop.

In the opening chapter, I emphasised that management is about relationships and that you, inevitably, create a relationship with each person that you manage. If your interactions with one of your team are mainly of the Critical Parent–Adapted Child variety, you will create a very different type of relationship than if you seek to establish Adult–Adult transactions as the norm.

Once again, I don't wish to be naïve. In any transaction, you can only invite someone to join you from their Adult ego state – you cannot compel them. Some people are lazy, or lack confidence, or have grown used to operating from an Adapted Child ego state in the workplace. If one of your team isn't willing or able to operate from Adult, you won't be able to establish an Adult–Adult relationship with them.

A less common pattern of transactions within a team is that the manager operates from Nurturing Parent, seeking to overprotect someone or failing to address problematic behaviour or poor performance. This again runs the risk of stimulating an Adapted Child response where a report doesn't take proper accountability for their contributions.

There are times when it's appropriate to operate from any one of the five ego states. For example, being in Free Child is a useful state for brainstorming ideas. Being in Nurturing Parent might be appropriate when supporting a colleague going through a really tough time. However, it's generally the case that operating from Adult, and inviting the other party to respond from their Adult, is more likely to be productive and enjoyable.

You might like to reflect on the situations where you yourself find it natural and easy to operate from your Adult ego state – where you're thinking logically, where you're aware of your own and other people's emotions, and where you're able to contribute effectively to the task in hand. And also on those situations where you operate from a Child or Parent ego state. What is going on – perhaps within yourself or perhaps stimulated by the behaviour of another person – that leads you into such an ego state? And, if it's appropriate, what might you say or do differently if you were operating from Adult?

> **RESOURCE**
>
> The 'Drivers Tool' (Crowe Associates Ltd): www.crowe-associates.co.uk/coaching-tools/the-drivers-tool/

Another idea in TA is the notion of *drivers*. A driver is a habitual way of behaving that has been shaped by your upbringing or childhood experiences. Five common drivers are:

1. be perfect!
2. be strong!
3. try hard!
4. please others!
5. hurry up!

There are advantages and disadvantages in each of the drivers. For example, there may be times when having a '*be perfect!*' driver helps you to deliver great results. However, if you always have to do a perfect job, you will create a lot of unnecessary pressure on yourself.

Having read more about each of the five drivers, you might reflect on which are your own drivers – and what you might do to harness them effectively.

References

Berne, E (1964) *Games People Play*. New York: Ballantine Books.

Harris, T (1969) *I'm Ok, You're Ok*. New York: Harper & Row.

Chapter 3: C
COACHING AND MENTORING

What comes to mind when you think of the word *coach*? Many people think first of a sports coach – maybe the manager of a football team, or perhaps a golf or tennis instructor. Others may think of a person who coaches someone to play a musical instrument or to pass their GCSE or A level exams.

I have had tennis and golf lessons in the past. I was pleased to receive some specific instructions on, for example, how to serve or how to play a bunker shot. And the instructions improved my game. As a line manager, you may wish to give clear instructions to your people on what you want them to do and how you want them to do it. This might be invaluable and entirely appropriate, particularly if the other person lacks relevant experience, skills or knowledge.

I find it useful to think of a spectrum of behaviours that can be used by someone to coach another. The spectrum runs from directive actions at one end to non-directive at the other. Table 3.1 show a list of ten behaviours, all of which may be useful depending on the situation.

Table 3.1 A spectrum of directive to non-directive coaching behaviours

DIRECTIVE
Instructing
Giving advice
Offering guidance

Table 3.1 (Continued)

Making suggestions
Giving feedback
Summarising an extended piece of conversation
Paraphrasing by rephrasing the client's words
Reflecting back using the client's own words
Asking open questions that raise awareness
Listening to understand
NON-DIRECTIVE

At the directive end of the spectrum lie behaviours such as giving instructions, offering advice or guidance, and making suggestions. When you're operating from the directive end, you're pushing a solution or idea of your own. You're telling someone what to do. On the other hand, at the non-directive end of the spectrum are behaviours such as listening to understand, asking open questions to help the other person explore, and playing back to them your understanding of what they've been saying – these are the three conversational skills in my definition of coaching below. You're seeking to draw out solutions or ideas from them. You're asking rather than telling.

There are times when it's helpful – perhaps essential even – to be directive. For example, when time is very limited, when someone lacks knowledge or skill, or when they're doing something that's unsafe. It may be that you are aware of important or strategic issues that are confidential and are not known to more junior staff. Giving someone the answer is also quicker, certainly in the short run. Note that, if you want to give direction, you need to know or be able to work out the right answer.

There are other times when it's important to let the other person work out the answer for themselves. As an illustration, they may be thinking through which of two job offers to accept – enabling them to explore the pros and cons of both may be more helpful than telling them which one you think they should choose. It's they who will be living with the consequences of their choice, perhaps for a long time. And they're more likely to be motivated by a course of action that they themselves have chosen.

My approach to coaching is primarily non-directive, which is reflected in the final two lines of my own definition of coaching:

Coaching is a relationship of rapport and trust in which the coach uses their ability to listen, to ask questions and to play back what the client has communicated in order to help the client to clarify what matters to them and to work out what to do to achieve their aspirations.

(Thomson, 2023)

I see my role as a coach as helping the client to work out what to do – it's not for me to tell them what to do. I draw on the conversational skills of listening to understand, asking mainly open questions, and playing back my understanding of what the other person has been saying – these are behaviours at the non-directive end of the spectrum.

Deciding whether to be directive or not is a choice. If, as a line manager, you want to coach someone who works for you, then it's important to be clear when you want to be directive and when you want to be non-directive – and also why you're making that choice.

You may find the idea of the coaching dance, summarised in Table 3.2, a useful guide for moving skilfully between being directive and being non-directive.

Table 3.2 The coaching dance

Directive	Non-directive
Manager-centred	Employee-centred
Pushing solutions or ideas	Pulling out solutions or ideas
Telling	Asking
Giving feedback	Generating feedback

In the spectrum of behaviours set out in Table 3.1, I placed *Giving feedback* somewhere in the middle. As an illustration of the coaching dance, it's useful to distinguish between *giving* feedback – when you tell the other person what you think they did well or less well – and *generating* feedback – when you ask them what they themselves think they did well or less well. It's often the case that they can assess clearly their performance, and you don't need to add anything. However, if they're missing some important points, you can move to the directive end of the spectrum and tell them your own observations or judgements. I shall look at giving and generating feedback in Chapter 47.

Mentoring

Another approach to supporting the performance or development of someone is mentoring. There aren't agreed definitions of the terms *coaching* and *mentoring*, and they are often confused or assumed to mean the same thing. Here is my own definition of mentoring (Thomson, 2023):

> *Mentoring is a relationship in which the mentor draws on their experience, expertise and knowledge to support and guide a less experienced person in order to enhance their performance or encourage their development.*

Comparing my two definitions, I'm positioning mentoring as being more towards the directive end of the spectrum. A useful mentor has relevant experience and knowledge that they are willing to share judiciously with their mentee – and it's their experience that makes them a suitable mentor. However, I think that a really good mentor can also operate non-directively, appreciating that there are times when it may be more useful to allow their mentee to work things through than to tell them what they think.

One way in which I draw upon the idea of the coaching dance is when a client asks me what I think. I often reply by saying that I'm willing to tell them what I think but, first, I'd like to hear their thoughts. If you're acting as a mentor, this might be a useful tactic. (That last sentence is a suggestion, from the directive end of the spectrum!)

> **RESOURCE**
>
> The Leader as Coach (Herminia Ibarra and Anne Scoular, *Harvard Business Review*): https://br.org/2019/11/the-leader-as-coach
>
> In this article, Herminia Ibarra and Anne Scoular discuss how the role of a manager has moved from a command-and-control approach to that of being a coach.

Reference

Thomson, B (2023) *Coaching from A to Z and Back Again*. St Albans: Critical Publishing.

Chapter 4: D

DELEGATION AND MICROMANAGEMENT

A manager is, by definition, someone who achieves results through other people. Hence, the ability to delegate work to others is a vital skill for any manager.

There are various reasons why someone may fail to delegate effectively or often enough. They might reckon that it's quicker to do the task themselves than to explain it to someone else. They might think they are the only person who can do the task well – which may or may not be a true assessment. They might not trust others. They might feel guilty about adding to the workload of others. They may keep to themselves work that is particularly interesting or likely to get the attention of senior management.

While some of these reasons might be valid reasons not to delegate something, there are a number of benefits in being able to delegate effectively. Good delegation saves time, freeing the manager up to do other things – perhaps to address more strategic issues or perhaps simply to have a better work–life balance. It might be viewed as an investment – taking time to explain something clearly can save more time in the long run.

Delegation gives the other person the opportunity to take on a challenge, and hence supports the development of their capability and their confidence. Taking on an interesting and challenging task can be motivating. When effective delegation becomes the norm within a team, it can help to create a culture of empowerment. And a manager who delegates effectively may be laying the platform for someone to succeed them or, more generally, to rise through their organisation.

Here are some guidelines on how to delegate a task successfully.

- Check that it's appropriate to delegate this task to someone else – some things do need to be done by you.
- Decide who is the best person (or group of people) to delegate the task to.
- Explain clearly what you're asking them to do. It can be useful to ask them to play back to you their understanding of this – it's what they understand that matters, not what you hoped they'd understand.
- You may need to be specific about things like deadlines, resources, constraints and the quality you are seeking.
- Unless the person is a novice, don't tell them how to do the task. Let them use their initiative and creativity. The US general George Patton offered this advice: *'Never tell people how to do things. Tell them what you want them to achieve and they'll surprise you with their ingenuity'* (BrainyQuote, nd).
- Delegation isn't abdication. You will need to monitor progress appropriately, and also to be available to offer support if necessary.
- After the task has been completed, you may wish to help the person to review how they did to draw out learning and lessons for future tasks.
- Say *'thank you'*.

I find the follow checklist of 4 Cs a useful guide for delegating a task to someone.

1. Are they *clear* about what you're asking them to do?
2. Are they *capable* – perhaps with some training or support – of doing it?
3. Are they *confident* about taking it on?
4. Are they *committed* to doing the task?

You need to be able to tick all four in order to delegate effectively. And, depending on where the gap is, you need to intervene in different ways.

First of all, the person to whom the task is being delegated needs to be clear what you are asking them to do. As noted earlier, it's their clarity not yours which matters.

Second, if the person isn't capable of doing the task, then – unless you're using this in part as a development opportunity and are able to give them the necessary support – it's unwise to delegate.

Third, they may be clear and capable but lack confidence. You may need to support them in various ways as they tackle the task. This can be very useful in building their capability and their confidence to tackle future challenges.

Finally, if the person is capable and confident but isn't committed, then you need a very different intervention if you want them to take on the task. What will give them the necessary motivation to carry out the task responsibly? This might be a financial incentive, the prospect of promotion, or something that speaks to their interests or values at a deeper level.

Micromanagement

Some managers are micromanagers who keep very tight control over all of the details of everything that they ask their people to do. They are constantly looking over people's shoulders, checking up on what they're doing. They may obsess over small details – for example, insisting on being copied into every email. When they delegate a task, they often spell out exactly how they want it to be done, leaving no room for someone to use their initiative or ideas. It may be that they don't trust anyone to do the job as well as they themselves would. Underlying their behaviour may be feelings of anxiety or insecurity.

Micromanagers don't know how to – or perhaps are unwilling to – delegate effectively. They create an environment where people are constrained, overdependent on the boss, and demotivated. Micromanagers suck energy and confidence from people, creating a culture where people aren't proactive and don't take responsibility.

I recall two directors from the time when I worked in management development in the energy industry. Richard was the director in charge of all of the operations of the gas transportation network in Britain. From time to time, I needed to speak to him to ask for his support with a development initiative. I could always get time with him within a day or two, and he was always helpful. When I went to his office, his desk was clear. He was running a complex operation and leading the work of literally thousands of people. He knew his role, he was strategic, and he could delegate effectively.

At the time I reported to a boss who was a micromanager, and she in turn reported to the HR director who was also a micromanager. I had a proposal for a mentoring scheme – something which I'd introduced successfully in a previous organisation. I knew well what I was doing. It took months to get the approval of my boss – and more months before I could sit down with the HR director to talk through the scheme. Their involvement added little or nothing to the proposal, but simply caused delay. I left the organisation not long afterwards.

In an article called 'Why People Micromanage', Ron Ashkenas writes:

> *Over the past few decades I've worked with hundreds of managers, and many complain that they work for micromanagers. But strangely I don't recall anyone who ever admitted to being one.*
>
> (Ashkenas, 2011)

You might like to reflect on whether or not you sometimes micromanage!

> **VIDEO**
>
> Effective Delegation (Naval Facilities Engineering Systems Command, 2020): www.youtube.com/watch?v=b-fTSOjaNl8
>
> This six-minute video discusses the importance of delegation and offers a number of tips on how to delegate effectively.

References

Ashkenas, R (2011) Why People Micromanage. *Harvard Business Review*, 15 November. [online] Available at: https://hbr.org/2011/11/why-people-micromanage (accessed 27 February 2024).

BrainyQuote (nd) George S. Patton Quotes. [online] Available at: www.brainyquote.com/quotes/george_s_patton_106027 (accessed 7 March 2024).

Chapter 5: E
EMOTIONAL INTELLIGENCE

As a manager, your words, decisions and actions have a big impact on the people who work for you – both on what they do and also on how they feel. This quote from Carl W Buehner (which is often attributed to Maya Angelou) illustrates how deeply you might influence the feelings of others (Quote Investigator, nd):

They may forget what you said – but they will never forget how you made them feel.

The idea of emotional intelligence sits at the heart of managing yourself and your relationships with the people whom you lead. Throughout the book I shall be emphasising the importance of what are sometimes called the 'soft skills' of management. In reality, developing and deploying soft, interpersonal skills is often much more difficult than 'hard' skills such as setting objectives, creating a plan and measuring outputs. Someone who is emotionally intelligent is well-equipped to build strong relationships – with their team, with their bosses and with peers and clients. This can enable them to manage, to influence and to negotiate successfully. Emotional intelligence gives you leverage.

In a paper published in 1990, Peter Salovey and John Mayer defined emotional intelligence as the ability to monitor one's own and others' feelings and emotions, to discriminate among them and to use this information to guide one's thinking and actions.

The term was popularised and entered mainstream business thinking in the mid-1990s with the publication of Daniel

Goleman's bestselling book, *Emotional Intelligence: Why it Can Matter More Than IQ.*

Figure 5.1 is a simple diagram which captures the four key aspects of emotional intelligence.

Figure 5.1 A framework for emotional intelligence

	Self	Others
Responsibility	*Self-management*	*Social skills*
Awareness	*Self-awareness*	*Empathy*

There is a useful equation in the world of coaching:

Awareness + Responsibility = Performance

In other words, someone who is aware of what they need to do and who takes responsibility for action will perform — whatever performance means in that context. It might be making a sales call, finishing a report, managing a team or hitting a golf ball.

Self-awareness

Emotional intelligence starts with self-awareness — being aware of how you yourself are feeling at any moment in time. It can be very useful to be able to put a name to whatever you're feeling, often with a single word. For example:

- I'm angry;
- I'm happy;
- I'm beginning to get upset;

- I'm confused now;
- I'm confused and upset;
- I'm excited.

I find that, when I ask someone how they're feeling, they often tell me what they're thinking.

- I feel it's a good idea;
- I feel it won't work.

Note that if you can insert the word *that* after *I feel* without changing the meaning of the phrase (as in the last two examples), then it's almost certainly a thought rather than a feeling.

An important aspect of self-awareness is knowing what really matters to you. It's useful to spend time reflecting upon and clarifying your own answers to questions such as these:

- What are my values?
- What motivates me?
- What do I believe about myself?
- What do I believe about other people?
- What are my goals, both short term and long term?

Self-management

Being aware of how you're feeling is the first step in emotional intelligence. You then need to take responsibility for what you will do as a result of that feeling. As an illustration, let's imagine that you're feeling angry in a meeting. It might be disastrous to show that you're angry – perhaps it would damage some delicate relationships. Alternatively, it might be useful to say that you're angry – and perhaps to explain why. You might say something along the lines of *'I'm feeling angry because we're not doing what we promised to do'*. To behave with emotional intelligence is to make wise choices about how to respond when your emotions are stirred. The preface of Goleman's book contains this quote from Aristotle which illustrates well this aspect of self-management:

> *Anyone can become angry – that is easy. But to be angry with the right person, to the right degree, at the right time, for the right purpose, and in the right way – that is not easy.*
> (Aristotle, in Goleman, 1996)

Empathy

The third area of emotional intelligence is awareness of how the other person is feeling – appreciating their perspective and concerns. The word that's often used here is *empathy* – being able to see the world from the point of view of the other person, recognising what really matters to them. Tuning into the reality of the other person may involve paying attention to their non-verbal communication. The look on their face or the tone of their voice may tell you something very different from the words that they speak. Awareness of others also extends to understanding what is going on within a group of people.

Empathy is not the same as sympathy. When you sympathise with someone, you are imagining how you would feel if you were in their position. You might express genuine feelings of pity or sorrow, and perhaps offer well-meaning but glib reassurance. You might say things like:

- I'm sorry to hear that;
- I know how you feel;
- I'm sure it will work out okay.

When you empathise, you are trying to understand how the other person is experiencing the situation that they are in. You acknowledge their reality, and seek to build some form of connection. You might say things like:

- It sounds like you're having a really tough time;
- I imagine that you're struggling with this;
- Let me know if there's any way I can help.

Social skills

As you become aware of how the other person is feeling, you then have a choice as to what you do in response. You might comment on or ask a question about what they've been saying. Or you might decide that now is not the time to explore but that you will enquire in a day or two. And there may be times when it's better to say nothing and move on. An emotionally intelligent person has a range of social skills that enable them to respond appropriately and successfully to a wide range of people and situations.

To show your appreciation of someone's situation, it can often be helpful simply to play back to them what you've heard or picked up. I find it useful to add a qualifying phrase to indicate that my playback is tentative rather than definitive. For example, I might say something along the lines of *'It sounds as though you're worried about the new arrangements'*. Or, *'I'm wondering if you're confused about what's expected of you'*. This gives them space to amend or reject my playback. Playing back reasonably accurately what matters to the other person helps to build the relationship.

In his article *What Makes a Leader?* Daniel Goleman writes:

> *Social skill is the culmination of the other dimensions of emotional intelligence. ... A leader who cannot express her empathy may as well not have it at all. And a leader's motivation will be useless if he cannot communicate his passion to the organization. Social skill allows leaders to put their emotional intelligence to work.*
>
> (Goleman, 2004)

VIDEO

Daniel Goleman Introduces Emotional Intelligence (Big Think, 2012): www.youtube.com/watch?v=Y7m9eNoB3NU

In this five-minute video Daniel Goleman explores a number of aspects of emotional intelligence.

References

Goleman, D (1996) *Emotional Intelligence: Why it Can Matter More Than IQ*. London: Bloomsbury.

Goleman, D (2004) What Makes a Leader? *Harvard Business Review*, 82(1): 82–92.

Quote Investigator (nd) They May Forget What You Said, But They Will Never Forget How You Made Them Feel. [online] Available at: https://quoteinvestigator.com/2014/04/06/they-feel/ (accessed 7 March 2024).

Salovey, P and Mayer, J (1990) Emotional Intelligence. *Imagination, Cognition and Personality*, 9(3): 185–211.

Chapter 6: F
FIERCE CONVERSATIONS

In her book *Fierce Conversations* the American executive coach Susan Scott (2002) explores how to engage in honest conversations that get to the heart of the matter. By *fierce* she does not mean aggressive but rather robust, passionate, eager.

Conversations that get to the heart of the matter, that surface assumptions and explore different perspectives, take time. They might seem like an indulgence in today's fast-paced world where people are very busy. However, the conversations that don't get to the heart of the matter in the end take up far more time because the decisions and actions 'agreed' in these conversations don't address the full reality of the situation. Scott (2002) writes that, *'fierce conversations often do take time. The problem is, anything else takes longer'*.

As a manager, the conversations that you have – and the conversations that you avoid – shape the relationship you have with each of the people who report to you and with your team. Scott (2002) observes that, *'The conversation is not about the relationship, the conversation is the relationship'*. And, in the words of the poet David Whyte: *'The core act of leadership must be the act of making the conversations real'* (Transformative Conversations, 2019).

A framework for a conversation

Here is a simple four-step framework that you might use to prepare for and then have a constructive conversation. The four steps are:

1. preparing;
2. opening;
3. discussing;
4. ending.

Preparing

It is useful to spend some time before a conversation thinking about what you'd like to achieve, what is likely to be important for the other person, and what might be difficult or challenging. You may find these questions useful.

- What do I want for me?
- What do I want for the other person?
- What do I want for our relationship?

Opening

At the start of a conversation, it can be helpful to spend a little time on some general chit-chat, showing interest in the other person. *How was your holiday? How are the family?* It's also valuable – and more important – to agree clear objectives for the conversation. On some occasions you, or the other party, might be dictating these objectives. At other times it may be essential to agree jointly the objectives for the conversation. It can be helpful to write these objectives down.

Discussing

This is the meat of the conversation where you jointly explore issues, discuss problems, consider solutions and agree actions. The skills I shall be looking at next – listening, questioning, playing back and voicing – are required throughout this discussion.

Ending

Not all conversations end with agreement or action plans. However, if you have agreed actions and next steps, it's very useful to summarise these explicitly.

- Who will do what by when?
- When shall we review progress or meet again?

These points are usefully captured in writing, and perhaps circulated afterwards.

Four conversational skills

There are four key skills that are invaluable if you wish to engage in conversations that get to the heart of the matter. The first three – listening, questioning and playing back what has been said – are all about understanding the point of view of the other person. The fourth skill is voicing – the ability to state clearly your own point of view. Let's look briefly at each of these. I shall discuss them further in later chapters.

Listening

Listening is an active process – it's much more than sitting passively while the other person talks. It requires concentration, and hence it can be tiring. I like to distinguish between *listening to respond* and *listening to understand*. The latter is much more useful – while the former is much more common!

When you are listening to respond, you're thinking about what you're going to say – which is often to disagree with the other person – and, hence, you're not paying full attention to what they're saying. In contrast, when you're listening to understand, your concentration is wholly on the words, and perhaps the non-verbal signals, of the other. Note that when you understand someone's point of view, that does not mean that you necessarily agree with it.

Questioning

I like to distinguish between *closed* and *open* questions. Closed questions can be answered *yes* or *no*, or perhaps with a one-word answer. Open questions, on the other hand, invite a much fuller reply. Open questions begin with words like *What?* or *How?* or phrases such as *To what extent?* or *In what ways?* The answer to an open question is likely to reveal much more than a closed question.

One question that I often ask is some form of *What else?* For example, *What else is important to you?* Or, *Who else do we need to consult?* This often generates more information or ideas, and a fuller understanding.

Playing back

The third conversational skill is to play back your understanding of what the other person has been saying. I often use a *summary* of an extended piece of conversation to share my understanding of the other person's position or argument. This helps to check for mutual understanding. And it shows that I've been paying attention, which can help to build rapport in the relationship.

I also play back in two other ways. I will sometimes *paraphrase* a particular point, changing their words into a different formulation. There is a risk here that I get this wrong, and so at times I simply *reflect back* their exact words. There can be a power and meaning in the exact phrase or metaphor used by the other person.

Voicing

While it is important to use the first three skills to explore and understand the other person's perspective, it is also essential to be able to put forward your own point of view. Voicing is the ability to state clearly what you think and the reasons that underlie your thinking. Being able to share your thoughts and feelings, your aims and concerns, and perhaps your hopes and fears, is vital in order to search for an agreement that will satisfy your needs.

This ability to voice – to ask for what you want or need – is at the heart of behaving assertively. Tone of voice or body language may be important here. Speaking loudly and aggressively, on the one hand, or meekly and passively, on the other hand, can be counterproductive.

> **VIDEO**
>
> Susan Scott – What to be Mindful of and How 'Fierce Conversations' Helps your Business (Vistage, 2011): www.youtube.com/watch?v=wQPCM40fb-s
>
> In this four-minute video Susan Scott explores the power of – and the benefits of – engaging in fierce conversations with the people around you.

References

Scott, S (2002) *Fierce Conversations*. London: Piatkus.

Transformative Conservations (2019) Leading Teams Requires Interactive Conversations. 11 August. [online] Available at: www.transformativeconversations.com/blog/leadership-is-conversations/2019-09-11 (accessed 7 March 2024).

Chapter 7: G
GROWING PEOPLE

The title of my first book was *Growing People*, with the subtitle *Learning and Developing from Day to Day Experience*. The book explored how a manager can support the development of their people by offering them appropriately challenging experiences and helping them to reflect upon and learn from these experiences. In the opening paragraph of *Growing People* I state the philosophy that is the foundation of my approach to learning and development.

> *I strongly believe that deep and sustained learning – that is, becoming able to do something you couldn't do before – only comes through experience. Experience on its own isn't enough, however. You need to reflect on and make sense of your experience to create knowledge, and this knowledge deepens when you apply it in new situations.*
>
> (Thomson, 2006)

You can view this as a learning cycle:

Figure 7.1 The cycle of learning from experience

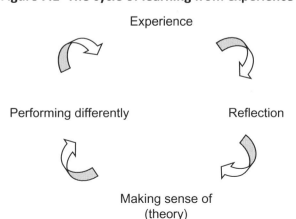

The learning cycle in Figure 7.1 is my rewording of David Kolb's cycle of learning from experience. The terms he uses are *Concrete experience*, *Reflective observation*, *Abstract conceptualisation* and *Active experimentation* (Kolb, 1984).

In his book *High Flyers* Morgan McCall (1998) writes: *'The principle is simple: people learn most by doing things they haven't done before.'* Hence, if you wish to develop the staff who work for you, it's essential to identify what experiences they need at this point in their development. Something which is well within their comfort zone won't be developmental, while something that is way beyond their comfort zone will be inappropriate and may cause stress and anxiety.

In many organisations there is a performance and development review process. This is often based on an annual conversation which a manager has with each member of their staff. This is frequently something of a ritualistic and token encounter where the focus is on completing and returning the paperwork to the human resources department. The document is then filed away, possibly to be retrieved 12 months later. (I shall look at performance and development reviews in Chapter 16.)

A much more effective way of approaching such a meeting is to view it as a conversation which is an honest discussion of performance – what the person has done well and less well over the past year – and an exploration of what development goals and actions are appropriate. Honest and constructive feedback on performance is an essential part of the process.

In regard to the development part of the process, you might move to the non-directive end of the coaching spectrum and structure the conversation around a series of open questions which put the reviewee at the heart of the review; the following questions provide examples.

- What do you regard as your strengths, both technical and behavioural?

- What do you see as your weaknesses, both technical and behavioural?
- What are your aspirations?
- What new experiences or challenges will support your development?
- How can I, as your manager, assist with these?

It is useful to end such a discussion with a clear statement of development goals and an action plan to pursue these. As suggested above, an important part of the action plan may be new experiences which the reviewee now needs. These might link to the performance objectives which the review has identified. So, for example, tackling a new piece of work or leading a new project might feature. It might be appropriate for the individual to be seconded to another part of the organisation. Or it could be that it's now time for them to find a new role, either within or beyond the organisation.

A common outcome of a development review is that the individual will take part in a training programme of some kind. There may be an internal learning and development team who deliver programmes and courses within the organisation. These might be face-to-face workshops or online programmes, or some blend of both. Or perhaps it would be valuable to take an external course, which might or might not lead to some form of qualification or accreditation. This will usually cost more, and can be a sign that the individual and their progress is valued highly by the manager and the organisation. (I recall how pleased I felt when my boss agreed to me attending a substantial external coach training programme – this turned out to be a vital step in my own career development.)

Another potentially valuable development mechanism for the individual is to work with a coach or mentor. In Chapter 3 I looked at the distinction between coaching and mentoring, suggesting that a mentor is someone with relevant experience and knowledge who may use this to support and guide the mentee, whereas a coach will use a primarily non-directive approach to help the individual to explore and address issues and challenges. Both forms of support can be valuable, and it's worth discussing what will best help the individual. It may be that you as the line manager will take the role of mentor and/or coach. Some organisations have internal mentoring or coaching schemes where members of staff have been identified – and hopefully trained – to take such a role. And, as with training programmes, it's possible that an external solution is appropriate. One difference between coaching and mentoring is that external mentors often take on the role without charging, seeing this as a way of giving something back to their profession or industry. Employing an external coach will cost money, sometimes a considerable amount. It is a significant investment to support the performance or development of someone.

Whatever interventions are agreed – on-job activities, participation in learning events, mentoring or coaching – it's very helpful if, as a manager, you later spend time with the individual helping them to review their experiences. This can help them to crystallise what they've learnt and identify what else they now need to do – that is, it helps them to go around the learning cycle. Moreover, it gives you feedback on what's worked or not worked, which may influence what you discuss in future development conversations with your people. Engaging in such conversations – about performance as well as development – throughout the year keeps the review process alive, and makes it less likely to be viewed as an annual ritual to keep the HR department happy.

I develop these ideas in later chapters. I look again at performance and development reviews in Chapter 16. Chapter 33, 'Talent management', discusses how to use developmental experiences as the basis for succession planning in an organisation. Chapter 47 considers how to give feedback to and how to generate feedback from an individual. And Chapter 50 extends the idea of the cycle of learning from experience to a cycle of development where offering people new and challenging experiences builds both their capability and their confidence.

> **RESOURCE AND VIDEOS**
>
> What is Experiential Learning? (Institute for Experiential Learning, nd): https://experientiallearninginstitute.org/what-is-experiential-learning/
>
> This link to the website of the Institute for Experiential Learning contains text and videos which explore the nature of experiential learning, the cycle of learning from experience, and nine styles of learning – each of us has preferences for some of these styles and underutilise others.

References

Kolb, D (1984) *Experiential Learning: Experience as the Source of Learning and Development*. Englewood Cliffs: Prentice-Hall.

McCall, M (1998) *High Flyers: Developing the Next Generation of Leaders*. Boston: Harvard Business School.

Thomson, B (2006) *Growing People: Learning and Developing from Day to Day Experience*. Oxford: Chandos.

Chapter 8: H

RON HEIFETZ AND ADAPTIVE LEADERSHIP

In their book *The Practice of Adaptive Leadership* Ron Heifetz, Marty Linsky and Alexander Grashow (2009) make a distinction between a technical problem and an adaptive challenge. A technical problem may be complex and critically important, but it can be solved using current know-how and ways of working. There are many challenges and problems in organisational life which can be addressed effectively by deploying expertise and managerial authority. Replacing a faulty heart valve during cardiac surgery is an example of a critical problem for which there is a known procedure that can be carried out by a suitably trained surgeon and support staff within the daily routines of a hospital.

An adaptive challenge, on the other hand, requires a solution that is beyond current capabilities and ways of working. In 2020, for example, nations, organisations and individuals faced the adaptive challenge of how to cope with the Covid-19 pandemic. Heifetz et al (2009) write:

> *The most common cause of failure in leadership is produced by treating adaptive challenges as if they were technical problems. ... Adaptive challenges can only be addressed through changes in people's priorities, beliefs, habits and loyalties.*

There is a three-stage process to tackle an adaptive challenge – and it's an iterative process rather than a linear one.

1. First, observe what is happening in the world and around you.
2. Second, interpret what is happening – you might come up with multiple hypotheses.
3. Third, intervene – design an intervention based on your observations and interpretations. This may involve trial and error, and learning from these.

This perhaps gives a misleading impression that it's straightforward. It can be difficult to identify in a timely fashion what are the critical trends and changes affecting your organisation or department. It may also be hard to develop an accurate and appropriate understanding of what you're noticing. And, by definition, it won't be possible to lift a suitable intervention off the shelf.

A metaphor that's relevant to the role of the leader is the notion of stepping off the dance floor and getting on the balcony. On the dance floor, you are in the midst of action, immersed in day-to-day operations. Knowing what is happening on the ground can be valuable. However, a leader also has to be able to step away from the detail in order to gain a wider, more strategic perspective. Going to the balcony helps you to consider what's really going on, what's emerging and what needs to be addressed. It's important to cultivate the habit of stepping back in this way.

Since there is no easy answer to an adaptive challenge, it may be necessary to experiment with different ideas and solutions. This might involve taking risks. It's important not to be wedded to a particular solution that you've identified, to be willing to fail and to remain open to other possibilities.

Heifetz et al (2009) write: '*Adaptive leadership is the practice of mobilizing people to tackle tough challenges and thrive.*' This may require changes in values, beliefs, roles, relationships and approaches to work. A leader needs to connect with the concerns and anxieties of the people they're trying to engage. This calls for emotional intelligence more than facts, figures and logic. They write that, *'If you are not engaged with your own heart, you will find it virtually impossible to connect with theirs'* (2009).

A further point that Heifetz and his colleagues make is the importance of purpose. They emphasise that it's vital to be clear about your own values and what you see as the purpose of your work if you are going to take the risks that are involved in tackling adaptive challenges. Moreover, it's also necessary to define a shared purpose that the people whom you're leading through change can buy into.

An adaptive leader recognises that they do not know everything and that they are not the only person capable of coming up with ideas. Rather than impose their solution, they engage with the people around them to tap into their expertise and creativity. They value diverse opinions. Dialogue is more useful than direction.

Wicked, tame and critical problems

Keith Grint (2022), who was a colleague of mine at Warwick Business School, offers a different, three-fold typology of problems which extends the two-fold typology above.

1. Tame problems are like technical problems – we know how to solve them using standard procedures.
2. Wicked problems are like adaptive challenges – we don't know how to fix these.
3. And critical problems – these are 'self-evident' crises that require an immediate response that isn't standard.

He suggests that tame problems require 'managers' to provide the solution or to delegate the problem to someone who can. Wicked problems require 'leaders' who engage others to address the challenge. And critical problems require 'commanders' who can coerce others to ensure that the crisis is handled. He makes the interesting observation that *'management was often regarded as relatively boring, by comparison with the allegedly more exciting world of leadership'* (Grint, 2022).

In regard to the Covid-19 pandemic, he suggests that this produced all three types of problem:

> *The most successful countries in the pandemic appear to have considered it a deeply wicked problem requiring collaborative leadership with importance* [sic] *aspects of tame problems (managing the vaccine rollout) and critical problems (coercing the population into lockdowns and quarantines).*
>
> (Grint, 2022)

You might like to reflect upon the challenges that arise for you in your role. My guess is that most fall into the category of technical or tame problems – you know how to address these and you may or may not have all the resources you'd like. In today's fast-moving business environment, there may be adaptive challenges or wicked problems that require you to step on the balcony and to engage others effectively to explore what might be done. And occasionally there may be a critical problem or crisis that requires you to use your authority, presence and influence to direct people firmly.

RESOURCE

Ron Heifetz: Adaptive Leadership (Creelman Research, 2009): creelmanresearch.com/wp-content/uploads/2020/09/Creelman2009vol2_5.pdf.pdf

This is a transcript of an interview by David Creelman where Ron Heifetz discusses Adaptive Leadership.

References

Grint, K (2022) Critical Essay: Wicked Problems in the Age of Uncertainty. *Human Relations*, *75*(8): 1518–32.

Heifetz, R, Linsky, M and Grashow, A (2009) *The Practice of Adaptive Leadership: Tools and Tactics for Changing Your Organization and the World*. Boston: Harvard Business Press.

Chapter 9: I
INFLUENCING AND POWER

One of the important behaviours that you need to engage in – as and when required – is to influence others to follow some course of action. As a line manager, you might take a command-and-control position and instruct someone who reports to you to do something. There are downsides to command and control – for instance, you might gain compliance but not commitment. In Chapter 3 I explored how to take a coaching approach in your role as a line manager, balancing telling people what to do with asking them for their ideas.

In many situations, however, you need to influence others without the formal authority of being their line manager. Influencing may be defined as *the ability to affect attitude, behaviour or outcomes*. On their website, the learning and development company Revolution describe four influencing styles (Revolution Learning and Development, nd). Let's consider the four styles in turn.

Persuading (*I propose...***)**

The persuading style uses data, logic and reasoning to present an argument or idea. It aims to explain clearly the rationale for your proposal. The tone is calm, direct and unemotional.

Asserting (*I want...***)**

The asserting style is more demanding. It aims to use control or pressure, stating firmly what you want and why. The tone is strong, clear and insistent.

Drawing (*What do you think...?*)

The drawing style invites the other party (or parties) into the conversation. It aims to build consensus and to make them feel part of the solution. The tone is relaxed, open and inviting.

Energising (*I believe...*)

The energising style seeks to enthuse and motivate others through your energy and passion. It aims to get others to share your enthusiasm and positivity. The tone is upbeat, engaging and expressive.

Note that Persuading and Asserting may be regarded as *Push* styles of influencing, seeking to move someone in a direction. Drawing and Energising, on the other hand, are *Pull* styles, aiming to make the other person feel involved and part of an idea.

As with many other aspects of interpersonal behaviour, it's useful to be able choose and then deploy the style that is most appropriate to the situation and most likely to lead to the outcome you are seeking. Since influencing is likely to be about getting the other party to shift, you need to choose a style which fits with their preferences, not yours. Some people will be influenced by a logical, factual analysis, while others are more likely to be swayed by a creative, enthusiastic approach. You might like to reflect upon which of the four styles you typically use and feel comfortable with – and which of the styles you rarely or never deploy.

One area where it's valuable to be able to influence effectively is in managing your boss or, more generally, managing upwards within your organisation. A foundation for managing upwards is to have a good reputation for delivering results. Being regarded as a trustworthy member of staff with a track record of performing well will make it more likely that you'll be able to sell your ideas to senior people.

To influence your manager, you need to appreciate the world from their perspective, and to identify – perhaps through experience of what does and doesn't work – what styles or tactics are effective in persuading them to buy into your ideas. I note at the end of the next chapter how you might take into account their personality preferences when considering how to present a proposal to your boss.

Power

In physics, power is the rate at which energy is transferred. Power equals energy divided by time. Power is essential in order to make anything move.

In organisational settings, the term *power* is often viewed negatively. In the words of the historian Lord Acton, '*Power tends to corrupt, and absolute power corrupts absolutely. Great men are almost always bad men*' (Acton Institute, nd).

However, power can be used constructively. Indeed, power is essential in order to make things move – in organisations as well as in physics. It is the ends to which power is being exercised that may be positive or negative – and judgement on whether the ends are desirable can vary from person to person.

John French and Bertram Raven (1959) identified five bases of power found in organisations, and Raven (1965) later added a sixth. As you read through the descriptions below, you might consider which of these forms of power you yourself possess within (and perhaps beyond) your organisation.

1. **Coercive power**

    This is the ability to force someone to do something – perhaps against their will. It may gain compliance without commitment, and might generate resentment.

2. **Reward power**

   This is the ability to give some form of reward to someone. This might be tangible (a monetary bonus, for example) or intangible (a word of thanks or praise, for example). A potential downside to the use of rewards is that people become accustomed to them, seeing them as entitlements which may no longer motivate. You might think of rewards as *carrots* and coercion as *sticks*.

3. **Legitimate power**

   This is power which derives from a position of authority or a role. A manager in a hierarchy or an elected official, for example, has legitimate power. If someone loses their position, they may well lose their power too.

4. **Expert power**

   This is power which is based on having knowledge, skill, expertise or experience that is relevant to a problem or challenge. It can enable someone to earn the trust of others and to be influential. A specialist in an organisation is likely to have some form of expert power.

5. **Referent power**

   Someone who has referent power is liked and respected as an individual. Their power derives from being seen as attractive or worthy. People with charisma or presence, and celebrities who are famous in some way, have referent power.

6. **Informational power**

   This is power which is based on having access to information which others don't have but need or want. It may be used to control or limit the flow of information that's required to get things done.

It's worth noting that coercive, reward, legitimate and informational power each derive from one's *position*. On the other hand, expert and referent power are *personal* forms of power that do not depend on your position in an organisation. Note too that you might combine different forms of power in order to influence people or events.

> **VIDEO**
>
> Leading With Influence: The 6 Power Bases (Heidrick & Struggles, 2016): www.youtube.com/watch?v=A3sTrfvMdo4
>
> In this four-minute video Brigadier General Bernard Banks discusses pros and cons of the six bases of power. He notes that the use of legitimate or coercive power may get compliance rather than commitment, and suggests that expert or referent sources of power are most likely to lead to commitment.

References

Acton Institute (nd) Lord Acton Quote Archive. [online] Available at: www.acton.org/research/lord-acton-quote-archive (accessed 7 March 2024).

French, J and Raven, B (1959) The Bases of Social Power. In Cartwright, D (ed) *Studies in Social Power* (pp 150–67). Ann Arbor: Institute for Social Research.

Raven, B (1965) Social Influence and Power. In Steiner, I and Fishbein, M (eds) *Current Studies in Social Psychology* (pp 371–82). New York: Society for the Psychological Study of Social Issues.

Revolution Learning and Development (nd) 4 Influencing Styles and How to Use Them. [online] Available at: www.revolutionlearning.co.uk/article/4-influencing-styles-and-how-to-use-them/ (accessed 27 February 2024).

Chapter 10: J

CARL JUNG AND THE MYERS–BRIGGS TYPE INDICATOR

In the previous chapter I noted the value of tailoring your approach to the other person when you're trying to influence them. One way to address this begins by being clear about your own and the other person's personality. The Myers–Briggs Type Indicator (or MBTI) is the most widely used personality profile in the world, and is one framework for thinking about personality – there are many others! The model was developed by Katharine Briggs and her daughter Isabel Briggs Myers and was based on the psychological theories of Carl Jung. It proposes that each of us is born with an innate preference on four dimensions of personality. Our behaviour might be modified by our experiences – for example, our education or the kind of work that we do – but the model considers that our underlying personality doesn't change. We can change our behaviour – indeed that's what flexing your approach entails – but we can't change our underlying personality.

MBTI dimensions

The MBTI has four dimensions. Let's look at these in turn. As you read the descriptions, you might reflect on where you would place yourself on each dimension.

The Extravert – Introvert dimension (E or I)

This dimension refers to where someone gets their energy from and where they prefer to focus their attention. Extraverts are energised by being with other people – they like to focus on the outer world of people and activity. Introverts recharge their batteries, as it were, by withdrawing into their inner world – they prefer to focus on their own inner world of ideas and experiences.

Extraverts tend to think out loud whereas Introverts like to think things through before speaking. One way of caricaturing this is that Extraverts speak first and maybe think later, whereas Introverts think first and maybe speak later. At a party, an Extravert will be comfortable having short conversations with many people, while an Introvert would prefer to have a few deeper one-to-one conversations.

The Sensing – Intuition dimension (S or N)

This dimension refers to how people prefer to take in information and what kind of information they like to pay attention to. People with a Sensing preference like to see the detail and want information to be precise and accurate. They like to take in information that is real and tangible – what is actually happening.

Someone with an Intuition preference is happy with the big picture only, and may get bored if you give them too much detail. They like to take in information by seeing the big picture, focusing on the relationships and connections between facts. They may value the abstract and theoretical rather than the concrete and practical.

The Thinking – Feeling dimension (T or F)

The third dimension of the MBTI reflects how people prefer to make decisions. Those with a Thinking preference use logic and analysis to work out what to do. When making a decision, they like to look at the logical consequences of a choice or action, or the costs and benefits. At work they are likely to be task focused.

People with a Feeling preference base their decisions on their values and convictions. They like to consider what is important to them and to others involved when making a decision. They wish to treat people as individuals, and fairness is more important than consistency. At work they may emphasise people rather than task.

The Judging – Perceiving dimension (J or P)

People with a Judging preference like to live in a planned, orderly way, seeking to regulate and manage their lives. Faced with a task, they are likely to make a plan with milestones and deadlines. They hate last-minute changes, and may become stressed by undue time pressure.

People with a Perceiving preference like to live in a flexible, spontaneous way, seeking to experience and understand life, rather than control it. They feel constrained by plans and are comfortable simply going with the flow. They dislike making a decision until they have to. When deadlines loom, they are energised by last-minute time pressures.

Type or trait?

The four dimensions interact with one another, and lead to a four-letter description of an individual's personality type – for instance, INTP or ESFJ. There are 16 possible combinations. I won't go into this in this chapter, but you can find out more in the book *Your Secret Self* by Barbara Cox (2016).

An underlying premise of the MBTI is that each of these dimensions is one of *type* rather than *trait*. To give a simple analogy, type means that you can be born right-handed or left-handed, but you can't be born ambidextrous. Similarly, you have an innate preference for Extraversion or Introversion, etc. I don't agree with this – I think each dimension is a trait, and people sit along a spectrum. For instance, someone might have a very strong preference for either Extraversion or Introversion, and someone else might be somewhere in the middle. I have a very clear preference for Introversion and Intuition on the first two dimensions, but I am more in the middle of the Thinking–Feeling dimension and the Judging–Perceiving dimension. My overall Type is INTP.

An important point to note is that MBTI is all about preferences – it's not about assessing ability. For example, there are some highly socially skilled Introverts and some emotionally unintelligent Extraverts. But Introverts will find it takes more energy to interact with others than Extraverts do.

Flexing your behaviour

If you wish to understand more clearly your own preferences, it would be useful to complete your MBTI profile. This is based on a self-report questionnaire, so the results depend on how you see yourself. This means that it can be affected by your recent experience – or maybe just how you're feeling on the day you complete the questionnaire. There are a number of websites where you can take a test for free; there are others where you pay a fee and receive more information; and a third possibility is to pay to take the test and receive individual feedback from someone accredited to do this.

Knowing your preferences, you can then consider how you might usefully flex your own behaviour. As an illustration, my strong preference for Intuition means that I'm usually happy with an overview and generally don't feel the need for detail. However, there are occasions when it's important for me to pay close attention to the detail. I can do this – but it takes me more of an effort than it would for someone with a clear Sensing preference.

As I noted at the beginning of this chapter, you may usefully modify your behaviour when trying to influence someone else. Let's imagine that the MBTI profile of your boss is ISTJ. If you're presenting a proposal to them, it will be important to include all of the relevant details (their S preference), the costs and benefits and rationale for the idea (their T preference) and an implementation plan with a clear timeline (their J preference). You might also send your proposal in writing to them in advance so that they have time to think carefully about it before your meeting – someone with an I preference likes to think things through carefully.

> **RESOURCE**
>
> The Myers–Briggs Assessment Test (Psychometric Success, 2024): https://psychometric-success.com/aptitude-tests/test-types/myers-briggs
>
> Here you can read more about the MBTI, including a bullet-point summary of each of the 16 types.
>
> As I mentioned, my own MBTI profile is INTP. The website offers this summary description:
>
> *Prefers own company (I)*
> *Pattern/possibility oriented (N)*
> *Decisions based on logic/reason (T)*
> *Flexible/adaptable (P)*
>
> It also adds, '*They can come across as condescending and intolerant to those who do not hold their views and can also be absent-minded when it comes to the finer details*'. My wife would certainly agree with the second of those points!

Reference

Cox, B (2016) *Your Secret Self: Understand Yourself and Others Using the Myers–Briggs Personality Test.* Gainesville: Windhorse Books.

Chapter 11: K

JOHN KOTTER: LEADERSHIP IS DIFFERENT FROM MANAGEMENT

John Kotter begins his classic *Harvard Business Review* article 'What Leaders Really Do' with the words, *'Leadership is different from management'* (Kotter, 2001). In his view, leadership is about *change* while management is about *complexity*. The differences between these two complementary activities are summarised in Table 11.1.

Table 11.1 Leadership and management

LEADERSHIP	MANAGEMENT
Coping with change	**Coping with complexity**
Setting a direction	Planning and budgeting
Aligning people	Organising and staffing
Motivating and inspiring	Controlling and problem-solving

Leadership

Kotter argues that today's volatile, competitive and uncertain business environment requires organisations to change and adapt in order to survive. And creating change calls for leadership. The first step in leading change is to *set a direction* by establishing a vision for the future and a strategy to achieve this. Kotter notes that creating a vision isn't a mystical process – rather, it involves gathering intelligence and creating a realistic strategy that serves the interests of key stakeholders such as customers, shareholders and employees. An effective vision isn't magic, and might actually be based on mundane ideas that are already well known.

The next step is to *align people* by communicating the new direction so that everyone who can help to implement the vision – or who can block it – understands and is committed to the strategy. An important factor here is credibility – whether people believe the message depends on factors such as the track record and integrity of the leader, the content itself and consistency between words and actions. Alignment also empowers people to use their initiative in ways that support the achievement of the vision.

To ensure that people move in the desired direction – perhaps in the face of obstacles – the leader needs to *motivate and inspire* them. This is not achieved by pushing them but rather by appealing to their basic needs, values and emotions – such as achievement and recognition, a sense of belonging and a desire for control. Involving people appropriately in decisions that affect them can help to give a sense of control and to motivate. It's also important to recognise and reward success.

Management

The emergence of large organisations in the twentieth century meant that businesses needed to develop processes to manage the resulting complexity. Good management was required to avoid chaos and to bring order, consistency and stability. Faced with the challenges of a complex business environment, organisations need to *make plans and allocate budgets*. In order to carry out plans effectively, managers establish goals and targets – often for the next month, quarter or year – and decide what resources and funds will be allocated to which projects. Planning aims to produce order, not change.

Managers pursue their plans through *organising and staffing*. They create structures and job descriptions, populate organisation charts with suitably competent people, provide training opportunities where required, delegate responsibilities and monitor performance and results.

Managers then ensure that plans are achieved by *controlling and problem-solving*. They monitor the achievement of results, identify deviations from plan and make adjustments if necessary to get back on track. There are control processes in place to set sensible targets for quality, to detect lapses and to respond quickly and appropriately to variations.

Kotter (2001) writes:

> *The whole purpose of systems and structures is to help normal people who behave in normal ways to complete routine jobs successfully, day after day. It's not exciting or glamorous. But that's management.*

Leadership and management are both necessary for organisations to succeed in today's complex and changing business environment. The activities are complementary. Strong leadership with weak management can produce chaos. Strong management without leadership can produce bureaucratic stagnation as the world changes.

Kotter notes that some organisations develop a culture of leadership in which they consciously develop people to become '*outstanding leader-managers*'. As I noted in Chapter 7 on 'Growing people', a vital aspect of this is to provide appropriately challenging experiences to develop people who have leadership potential. Kotter writes:

> *Leaders almost always have had opportunities during their twenties and thirties to actually try to lead, to take a risk, and to learn from both triumphs and failures.*
>
> (Kotter, 2001)

I'll return to this important topic in Chapter 33 on talent management.

Leading organisational change

The website of the Kotter organisation sets out an eight-step methodology for leading organisational change (Kotter, nd). The list below may give the mistaken impression that this is a linear process – in reality, the leader or leadership team may need to revisit some of the stages as the change unfolds. Kotter emphasises that these phases in total take a considerable amount of time, and that skipping some of the steps never produces a satisfying result.

1. Create a sense of urgency

Opening an honest dialogue about what's happening in the business environment or what your competitors are doing, for example, can create a shared sense that change is essential. This can inspire and motivate people to act in pursuit of a clear and compelling vision of the future.

2. Build a guiding coalition

Assemble a coalition of people who are committed – and have enough power and influence – to lead the change effort. These can come from different levels and functions within the organisation, and the source of their power might be due to their expertise or political importance or status. The coalition needs to operate as a team that is committed to enacting the change.

3. Form a strategic vision

Create a vision and a strategy to direct the change effort. Clearly communicating the vision helps people to understand why they're being asked to change, making it more likely to get their buy-in for the initiatives needed to implement the vision. And actions speak louder than words – it's important that those leading the change demonstrate the behaviours being asked of others.

4. Enlist a volunteer army

Large-scale change can only occur when massive numbers of people rally around a common opportunity. It's important to enlist the support of people at all levels who understand the need for the change, who see the value in the change, who want to help make it happen and who can influence the views of others in the organisation.

5. Enable action by removing barriers

Change initiatives often encounter obstacles. There may be individuals or groups who are resisting change, or there may be processes or structures which are getting in the way. It is important to identify and remove such roadblocks, clearing the way for people to innovate, to work across silos and to move the change forward.

6. Generate short-term wins

Early successes are motivating. It's useful to plan for and create quick wins by setting some manageable aims that are easy to achieve and visibly improve performance. This can also help to still the voices of critics who might block progress.

7. Sustain acceleration

It's important not to skip any of the steps. Rather, keep up the momentum of change by consolidating improvements, measuring progress and continuing to work towards the change vision. It can be tempting – and fatal – to declare victory prematurely after a few early successes.

8. Institute change

The values that underpin the vision should be reflected in day-to-day work. Make sure that systems and processes reinforce the vision. Embed the new behaviours until they are strong enough to replace old habits. This helps to ensure that the new mindsets and ways of working become part of the culture throughout the organisation.

> **VIDEO**
>
> The Perils of Confusing Management and Leadership (Dr John Kotter, 2012): www.youtube.com/watch?v=Dz8AiOQEQmk
>
> In this five-minute video John Kotter talks about the perils of confusing management and leadership.

References

Kotter (nd) The 8 Steps for Leading Change. [online] Available at: www.kotterinc.com/methodology/8-steps/ (accessed 27 February 2024).

Kotter, J (2001) What Leaders Really Do. *Harvard Business Review*, 79(11): 85–98.

Chapter 12: L
LEADING WITH LOVE

In Chapter 1 on authenticity, I suggested that knowing and accepting your authentic self sits at the heart of creating successful working relationships with the people that you manage. At various points in the book, I invite you to explore who you are as a manager and how you will draw upon yourself to lead others.

I came across the book *Leading with Love* by Karen and Chris Blakeley shortly after it was published in 2022. I shared its key ideas with our full-time MBA students. Many of them felt that the ideas were really useful, although some suggested that terms such as *Leading with Care* or *Leading with Compassion* might be more appropriate.

Karen and Chris Blakeley (2022) write that, '*learning to lead with love is primarily a work of remembering who we truly are at the deepest level of our psyche*'.

The subtitle of their book is *Rehumanising the Workplace*. In their view, for many people work has become a soulless activity and organisations are places where people feel disempowered and alienated. Leading with love is a way of countering this.

Love and power

The book is based on this carefully crafted definition of love:

> *To love is to act intentionally, in sympathetic response to others (including the sacred or the divine), to promote individual and overall well-being.*
>
> (Blakeley and Blakeley, 2022)

As I discussed in Chapter 9, *power* is a neutral term. Power is needed to make things move – in both the physical world and in the world of organisations. Martin Luther King said this on the relationship between power and love:

> *One of the great problems of history is that the concepts of love and power have usually been contrasted as opposites – polar opposites – so that love is identified with a resignation of power, and power with a denial of love. ... We've got to get this thing right. What is needed is a realization that power without love is reckless and abusive, and love without power is sentimental and anemic. Power at its best is love implementing the demands of justice, and justice at its best is love correcting everything that stands against love.*
> (King Institute, nd)

The Blakeleys argue that to lead with love requires wisdom, emotional and moral maturity, and self-awareness. An effective leader feels good about themselves, and the ability to accept and to love oneself is a foundation for being able to lead others with love. The book quotes Brene Brown who writes that, '*we can only love others as much as we love ourselves*' (Blakeley and Blakeley, 2022).

At the other end of the spectrum of psychological maturity are leaders who are '*egotistical, intimidating and manipulative*' (Blakeley and Blakeley, 2022). They may lead with fear rather than love.

How to lead with love

The book presents a model of how to lead with love as an image of a tree, with roots, a trunk and a canopy (the leaves and fruit). The roots are akin to deep, personal motivators; the trunk is about the formation of character; and the canopy is the expression of love in action. Here is how they develop the metaphor.

- **The roots:** outstanding leaders have clear values and a personal philosophy that guides their actions. They are also aware of what drives their ego. Like the roots of a tree, these deep values and principles are the source of the love which guides their decisions and actions. The capacity to love oneself is an important aspect of this.
- **The trunk:** these leaders learn how to prioritise their values, reflect on their practice and manage their ego needs. They have developed high levels of confidence based on self-awareness, reflexive learning and self-acceptance. The trunk represents the channel that connects their values and sense of self to their visible actions in the world – it enables them to align their actions with their intentions. Being vigilant around their egocentric drivers enables them to control their behaviour.
- **The canopy:** leading with love involves getting to know the individuals that they lead, their hopes, fears and ambitions. Outstanding leaders express kindness, build trust, use power with integrity, and coach and develop their people. The canopy of the tree – its leaves and fruit – represents the impact these leaders have on others and their well-being as they balance love and power.

To emphasise that leading with love requires *'a shift in consciousness rather than the development of a set of skills'*, the book introduces three terms – Re-sourcing, Channelling and Embodying – to convey the idea that it *'entails a new transformational perspective on the self, on others, and on the world'* (Blakeley and Blakeley, 2022).

- **Re-sourcing:** how do you choose to remember who you really are – your values, your beliefs, what motivates you – rather than acting in response to situational drivers? What can you do each day to re-source yourself?

- **Channelling:** to what extent are you able to act according to your values and intentions? Do you accept yourself or are you dominated too much by your inner critic?
- **Embodying:** how attentive are you being to the needs of others? What impact are you having on others? What is the quality of connection between you and others?

You might like to set aside some time to think through how you yourself would answer the questions above.

> **RESOURCE AND VIDEO**
>
> Leading with Love: Rehumanising the Workplace (Karen Cripps, *Leadership*, 2021): https://journals.sagepub.com/doi/full/10.1177/17427150211050439
>
> In this online article, Karen Cripps sets out a chapter-by-chapter summary of the book.
>
> Power at its Best is Love (Martin Luther King, Jr, 2017): www.youtube.com/watch?v=SsvSq5_vbL4
>
> You can hear Martin Luther King say the words quoted above on love and power in this one-minute video.

References

Blakeley, K and Blakeley, C (2022) *Leading with Love: Rehumanising the Workplace*. Abingdon: Routledge.

Brown, B (2010) *The Gifts of Imperfection: Let Go of Who You Think You're Supposed to Be and Embrace Who You Are*. Center City: Hazelden Publishing.

King Institute (nd) Where Do We Go From Here? Speech, 16 August 1967. Stanford. [online] Available at: https://kinginstitute.stanford.edu/where-do-we-go-here (accessed 7 March 2024).

Chapter 13: M
MANAGING MEETINGS

One of the main ways in which many people who work in organisations spend their time is in meetings. Some of these will be important and useful, some will be important but useless, and some will simply be useless. I have a personal *rule of three* in regard to some meetings that I'm expected to attend but which are largely useless. It would be politically unwise never to attend, but my attendance adds little or no value for me or others. So, I attend roughly one in three of these rituals.

If you are the person chairing a meeting, it's useful to think through what you need to do before, during and after a meeting.

Before the meeting

One of Stephen Covey's seven habits of highly effective people is '*Begin with the end in mind*' (Covey, 1989). It's very useful to be clear in your own mind what the purpose of the meeting is and what you want to achieve. Sharing information, gathering views or making a decision are very different purposes.

It's also useful to have an agenda which reflects the purpose of the meeting. This might be a formal agenda circulated in advance, or it might simply be a number of items in your own mind. Be realistic about how many items can be covered, and ensure that you don't leave the most important ones to the end (as you might then be running out of time).

Set a start time for the meeting. People will work out whether your meetings start on time or whether the convention is that it's okay to turn up ten minutes late. One thing I've noticed is that online meetings on Teams or Zoom, for example, are more likely to start on time than face-to-face meetings.

Let people know if you want them to do anything to prepare for the meeting – some will do this conscientiously and others won't! If some of those attending have an Introvert preference (see Chapter 10), they may well value having time to think things through before the meeting.

One important action that you might take before some meetings is to contact some of the key stakeholders to lobby and influence them.

During the meeting

Meetings are conversations. The four key conversational skills that I looked at in Chapter 6 on 'Fierce conversations' – listening to understand, asking open questions, playing back your understanding of people's views, and voicing your own views clearly – are valuable skills to help you manage meetings well.

As the chair of the meeting, you have the responsibility of managing the process of the meeting. You may need to pay attention to the dynamics within the room. You might have to encourage contributions from quieter or less confident participants, and perhaps to limit the contributions of more vocal people. Some people can talk a lot without saying anything useful! The way in which you chair meetings with your team shapes the relationships you have with each of them.

It can be challenging to argue persuasively for a particular point of view while at the same time facilitating the conversation. One possibility here is to ask someone else to take the chair when the discussion is about an issue that you feel strongly about.

You also need to manage the time, balancing the time given to each item on the agenda and ensuring that the meeting addresses all of the key items. Summarising effectively can be really useful in acknowledging contributions and punctuating the conversation so that you can move the meeting on.

It's important to capture key decisions and actions, noting who will do what by when. You may wish to ask someone else to take notes, freeing you to do some of the things I've been mentioning. To state the obvious, you need to choose someone whom you can trust to keep up with the discussion and record decisions accurately. I find it useful to close a meeting by checking that everyone understands what actions are down to them. And it's their understanding that matters, not what I hoped they'd understand.

After the meeting

Some meetings are formal, and the minutes circulated afterwards may be highly political documents where statements need to be carefully crafted – minutes might be referred to long after a meeting has taken place. And the views expressed by different participants might need to be shared very sensitively.

However, when the meeting is less formal, my own preference is simply to circulate a list of action points – who will do what by when – and perhaps one or two key messages. I like to do this as soon as possible after the meeting, often on the same day. When I leave this for a few days, I sometimes find it harder to recall some of the details – the illegibility of my handwriting doesn't help here!

It's also important to follow up on actions, to monitor appropriately that people are doing what was expected of them within the timescale agreed. You might also need to have follow-up conversations with people – perhaps to reassure, or to find out more about their views, or to support them in carrying out actions that the meeting has assigned to them. And you might need to have a tough conversation with someone whose behaviour or contributions during the meeting were unhelpful.

David Kantor's four-player model

David Kantor's four-player model (2012) describes four stances or roles that need to be taken for a fully effective conversation.

1. **Move** – someone has to put forward an idea or a proposal. (*Let's play tennis on Saturday.*)
2. **Follow** – it can be useful for others to support or to build upon such a Move. (*Shall I book a court for 10.00?*)
3. **Oppose** – it may be important for a Move to be challenged (*Some of us don't like tennis*) or for an alternative suggestion to be made (*I'd rather play golf on Saturday*). The latter is also a Move.
4. **Bystand** – this doesn't mean being silent – it can be useful to offer a comment on what's happening within the conversation. (*We haven't heard what Tom or Mary would like to do.*)

These roles are likely to be played by different participants in the conversation. It is important, however, that all four roles are played.

- Without Movers, there is no direction.
- Without Followers, there is no completion.
- Without Opponents, there is no correction.
- Without Bystanders, there is no perspective.

You might like to reflect on some of the meetings that you currently attend. Take some time to capture your thoughts on these questions.

- Which of David Kantor's four roles do you typically play?
- Which of the roles do you rarely or never play?

And, for the meetings that you chair:

- Which roles are generally not played by anyone in the meeting?

> **VIDEO**
>
> 7 Tips for Chairing a Meeting (Ontario Library Association, 2018): www.youtube.com/watch?v=lHFrerN7vCc
>
> This five-minute video offers seven practical tips for chairing a board meeting.

References

Covey, S R (1989) *The 7 Habits of Highly Effective People*. London: Simon & Schuster.

Kantor, D (2012) *Reading the Room: Group Dynamics for Coaches and Leaders*. San Francisco: Jossey-Bass.

Chapter 14: N

SAYING *NO*: MANAGING YOUR TIME

Many years ago I attended a time-management course that was delivered well and which I found very useful. The ideas shared in the course seemed to be at two levels. I explored some that were philosophical in nature where I considered in depth what was really important to each of us. And the facilitator shared a variety of tips on time management, such as how to use a Filofax effectively. (That gives you an idea of how long ago the course was!)

I think that a mark of a really good course is that you learn something which you are still using many years later. The most important idea that I took from the workshop is that the key to managing your time effectively is to know your priorities and to spend your time in ways which reflect those priorities.

In his bestselling book *The 7 Habits of Highly Effective People* Stephen Covey (1989) sets out seven habits to help people to live balanced and fulfilled lives. His third habit is '*Put first things first*'. Identifying and following your priorities is vital.

Covey makes the distinction between activities that are *urgent* and activities that are *important*. This leads to the 2 × 2 matrix shown in Figure 14.1. This is also known as the Eisenhower matrix – the US President Dwight D Eisenhower used the same idea to organise his workload and priorities.

Figure 14.1 The urgent–important matrix

	URGENT	NOT URGENT
IMPORTANT	Crises Pressing problems Deadline-driven projects Some meetings	Preparation Prevention Planning Relationship building Recreation Empowerment
NOT IMPORTANT	Interruptions Some phone calls Some mail or reports Some meetings Some 'pressing matters' Many popular activities	Trivia, busywork Junk mail Some phone calls Time wasters 'Escape' activities

Most people when they are faced with a critical deadline – something which is important and urgent – are good at attending to it. What really distinguishes people who are excellent at managing their time is that they focus on things which are *important but not yet urgent*. It is interesting to look at the items in the *important and not urgent* box – preparation and planning, building relationships and empowering others. These can be regarded as investments of time which will yield valuable dividends later. Recreation – the things you do to maintain your well-being – can also be seen as important but not urgent.

I've noticed that when I invite a workshop delegate or a coaching client to list the things that they do and then place them on the grid, people usually regard most of their activities as important. But, not everything can be top priority – by definition, some things are more important than others. If you want to manage your time effectively and strategically, then you need to clarify what you really do see as important. While you may need to fit in with the wishes of others, ultimately you decide what's important to you.

Moving from the more philosophical consideration of clarifying what's really important to a more practical action, here is one tip. It can be summed up in Covey's (1989) suggestion that: *'The key is not to prioritise what's on your schedule, but to schedule your priorities.'* So, book time in your calendar to tackle the more strategic things – like writing an important report, preparing a presentation, meeting the individuals who work for you or doing the things that simply help you to recharge your battery. Covey recommends organising your workload on a weekly, not a daily, basis. And, just because a meeting is in your calendar, it doesn't mean that it's important – or that you have to attend it.

Having put the important things in your calendar, you also need to make sure that you actually tackle them. Having good intentions is a useful first step, but it's not enough.

A word that I like to use when talking about time management is *ruthless*. By ruthless, I don't mean cruel or unfeeling. Rather, I mean having a very clear focus and determination. I think it's helpful to be ruthless when identifying and scheduling your priorities.

This means that there will be times when you need to say *no* to requests or invitations. There is a book in the literature on assertiveness which has the title *When I Say No, I Feel Guilty* (Smith, 1975). The ability to say *no* is an invaluable skill in both managing your time and in behaving assertively. This doesn't mean ignoring the needs of others, but rather is about balancing sensibly your own needs and the needs of other people. I shall explore assertiveness in the final chapter of the book.

The seven habits

I think that all seven of Covey's habits are useful guides. The first three habits listed below are concerned with personal effectiveness, the next three with interpersonal relationships and the final one is about constantly renewing the other habits.

1. **Be proactive.** Take responsibility for your life and your choices. Show initiative. Don't blame others or circumstances.
2. **Begin with the end in mind.** What do you want to be remembered for? What do you really, really want?
3. **Put first things first.** Identify and follow your priorities. This is the key to time management.
4. **Think win–win.** Look for agreements or solutions that are mutually beneficial. Seek to collaborate rather than compete.
5. **Seek first to understand, then to be understood.** Take time to listen to understand the other person's perceptions and priorities. Listen for feelings and meanings, not just facts and logic. Then express your own views clearly.
6. **Synergy.** Creative co-operation means that 1 + 1 can equal 3 or more. Honest communication and a valuing of differences mean that new possibilities can be created.
7. **Renewal.** Maintenance is essential. Keep the habits alive by continually attending to them, and by continually developing and renewing yourself.

> **RESOURCE**
>
> How to Say No to Others (and Why You Shouldn't Feel Guilty) (BetterUp, 2022): www.betterup.com/blog/how-to-say-no
>
> This article by Elizabeth Perry offers a rich set of ideas on:
>
> - why it is so hard to say no;
> - when you should say no;
> - why it's important to say no;
> - ten different ways to say no;
> - helpful tips on how to say no;
> - how to decide when to say no.

References

Covey, S R (1989) *The 7 Habits of Highly Effective People*. London: Simon & Schuster.

Smith, M (1975) *When I Say No, I Feel Guilty*. London: Bantam.

Chapter 15: O
IMAGES OF ORGANISATION

For many years I ran the Warwick Leadership Programme for academics, administrators and commercial managers working at the University of Warwick. On one occasion I recall introducing an exercise to explore metaphors as a way of understanding management and organisations. There were two academics from our Centre for Applied Linguistics who responded enthusiastically. And there were two engineers who gave each other a look as if to say *'Why on earth would anyone want to explore metaphors?'*

In his classic book *Images of Organization*, Gareth Morgan (1996) explores eight metaphors used to view organisations. Metaphor is much more than a matter of language. Not only do we speak in terms of metaphor, but we also think in terms of metaphor. And how we think shapes how we act. A metaphor is capable of capturing vividly a great deal of abstract and intangible information in a concise and memorable package. Note, however, that all metaphors are partial and are not literally true nor false. The value of a metaphor depends on the richness of the insights it generates.

In *Images of Organization*, Morgan

> *explores and develops the art of reading and understanding organizational life. It is based on a very simple premise: that all theories of organization and management are based on implicit images or metaphors that lead us to see, understand, and manage organizations in distinctive yet partial ways. ...*

The use of metaphor implies a way of thinking and a way of seeing that pervade how we understand our world generally.

(Morgan, 1996)

Organisations as machines

Morgan begins with the most common metaphor used to think about organisations – the organisation as a machine.

In this metaphor the organisation is viewed as made up of interlocking parts that fit together. When we draw a typical organisation chart, with a hierarchy of roles and reporting relationships, we are – generally unconsciously – using a machine metaphor of the organisation. When we think in terms such as improving efficiency, raising productivity, driving change, re-engineering, devolving responsibility or cascading objectives, we are using the machine metaphor. The machine metaphor is so deeply ingrained that many of us don't realise that we are using it or that there may be other ways of thinking about organisations.

Morgan writes:

Consider, for example, the mechanical precision with which many of our organizations are expected to operate. Organizational life is often routinized with the precision demanded of clockwork. People are frequently expected to arrive at work at a given time, perform a predetermined set of activities, rest at appointed hours, and then resume their tasks until work is over. In many organizations, one shift of workers replaces another in methodical fashion so that work can continue uninterrupted twenty-four hours a day every day of the year. Often, the work is very mechanical and repetitive. Anyone who has observed work in the mass-production factory or in any of the large 'office factories' processing paper forms such as insurance claims, tax returns, or bank checks will have noticed the machine-like way in which such organizations operate. They are designed like machines, and their employees are in essence expected to behave as if they were part of machines.

(Morgan, 1996)

Morgan points out that the machine metaphor works well under conditions where machines work well. These conditions include a straightforward task that needs to be replicated over and over, a stable environment and a context where the human parts are compliant and well behaved. In situations where precision, safety and clear accountability are required, mechanistic approaches can be very effective.

A mechanistic approach to organisations works less well when circumstances change. It can also have a dehumanising effect on employees, particularly those low down in the organisational hierarchy, who may feel that they are simply a *cog in the system*.

Organisations as organisms

Morgan's second metaphor views organisations as organisms – that is, as living systems existing in a wider environment and needing to adapt to changes in that environment. The organism metaphor has been widely employed over the past 70 years, and we are using it when we talk about corporate survival, product life cycles or organisational health checks. A SWOT analysis of an organisation's strengths and weaknesses and the opportunities and threats in its business environment is based on this metaphor.

Morgan introduces the organism metaphor by talking about different species of organisation in different environments:

Just as we find polar bears in arctic regions, camels in deserts, and alligators in swamps, we notice that certain

> *species of organization are better 'adapted' to specific environmental conditions than others. We find bureaucratic organizations tend to work most effectively in environments that are stable or protected in some way and that very different species are found in more competitive and turbulent regions, such as the environments of high-tech firms in the aerospace and micro-electronics industries.*
>
> (Morgan, 1996)

The machine metaphor viewed the design of organisations as a technical problem. Motivating people was largely a matter of paying the right rate for the job. In contrast, the organism metaphor recognises that people have complex needs that must be satisfied if they are to prosper and work effectively. A famous series of experiments at the Hawthorne Works in Chicago in the 1920s and 1930s identified the importance of social needs in the workplace. Psychological and human factors – such as autonomy, having choice and feedback – are important factors affecting morale and productivity.

The need to integrate both technical and human aspects of work and organisations – raising productivity, improving quality, enhancing job satisfaction and reducing employee absenteeism and turnover – is the basis of much that is done in human resource management. This dual focus sees an organisation as a *sociotechnical system*. Any change in the technical system – such as a restructuring or the introduction of a new technology – will have human consequences, and vice versa.

Morgan writes:

> *The focus on 'needs' also encourages us to see organizations as interacting processes that have to be balanced internally as well as in relation to the environment. Thus, we see strategy, structure, technology, and the human and*

managerial dimensions of organization as subsystems with living needs that must be satisfied in a mutually acceptable way. Otherwise, the openness and health of the overall system suffer.
(Morgan, 1996)

Morgan's other metaphors

In his book Morgan explores eight different metaphors for an organisation. The other six metaphors are:

1. Organisations as brains – where information is processed, learning takes place and intelligent action occurs. We draw on this metaphor when we talk about organisational learning.
2. Organisations as cultures – where *'values, ideas, beliefs, norms, rituals and other patterns of shared meaning'* (Morgan, 1996) guide organisational life. The culture of an organisation shapes the way people and groups interact with each other, with clients and with other stakeholders. (I look at organisational culture in Chapter 38.)
3. Organisations as political systems – an organisation can be viewed as a system of government, and hence politics is an essential part of organisational life. Differing interests lead to conflict, and power is the medium through which this is resolved. The ability to build coalitions is an important skill.
4. Organisations as psychic prisons – where people become trapped by their own thoughts, ideas and beliefs, or by the unconscious mind.
5. Organisation as flux and transformation – using ideas from complexity, chaos and paradox to view organisations as part of the ebb and flow of the whole environment.
6. Organisations as instruments of domination – how organisations may exploit employees and communities to further the selfish interests of elites.

> **VIDEO**
>
> What Are Morgan's 8 Organizational Metaphors? (Mike Clayton, 2021): www.youtube.com/watch?v=a60rsgbmw2c
>
> In this eight-minute video Mike Clayton summarises all eight of Morgan's metaphors.

Reference

Morgan, G (1996) *Images of Organization*. Thousand Oaks: Sage.

Chapter 16: P
PERFORMANCE AND DEVELOPMENT REVIEWS

In many organisations there is an annual process, often overseen by the HR department, in which every member of staff has an annual review meeting with their boss. This is sometimes a ritual which people – both the manager doing the review and the person being reviewed – comply with, don't enjoy and don't get much benefit from. The form gets filled in, returned to HR and forgotten about till the next round of the cycle 12 months later.

That is unfortunate. The review process offers the opportunity for meaningful conversation that explores constructively both the performance of the reviewee and their ongoing development and career aspirations.

The review meeting is often called an appraisal. The language here suggests that the manager is leading the process, telling the individual what they think is important. An alternative approach is to put the reviewee at the heart of the conversation, inviting them to take the lead on assessing their performance and their development needs.

In my view, the conversation is much more important that completing the paperwork. A meaningful review can play a significant part in shaping the relationship between manager and reviewee, ideally building a degree of mutual understanding, rapport and trust. One way to structure the session is to view it as a coaching conversation in which the manager asks the reviewee a series of open questions. This puts the reviewee at the centre of the process, an active participant rather than the recipient of messages. Of course, the manager will want to add their own views too. The framework in Figure 16.1 suggests that one way of structuring the conversation is to explore performance, past and future, and then development, past and future.

Figure 16.1 A framework for a performance and development review

	PERFORMANCE	DEVELOPMENT
PAST	What did you achieve over the last year?	How have you developed over the last year?
FUTURE	What are your objectives for the year ahead?	What are your development goals and plans for the future?

Past performance

Rather than beginning by telling the reviewee what the manager thought about their performance, an alternative is first to ask the reviewee questions that invite them to assess how well they think they performed. Here are some possible prompt questions.

- What were your key objectives for the last year?
- Which of these did you deliver successfully?
- Which objectives did you not meet (or not fully meet)? Why was that?
- Looking back, what would you like to have done differently?

Having encouraged the reviewee to reflect on their performance, it's important too for the manager to share their observations – particularly if the individual has an unrealistic view of their contribution or if they have missed something important. It might be that there is an issue of attitude or behaviour, rather than purely performance, that the manager needs to raise.

Future performance

In discussing future performance goals and targets, it's useful for the manager to set out the priorities of the team or department for the year ahead. This sets the context so that the conversation can then focus on how the reviewee can contribute to the department's objectives. There may be particular areas where they'd like to contribute – it may or may not be possible to accommodate this.

It is useful to capture specific objectives and perhaps deadlines for the reviewee. The degree of detail in which these are stated will vary, depending on the nature of the challenge – some goals can be stated in SMART language (specific, measurable, achievable, relevant and time-bound), while others may be more general or aspirational. It's also important too to discuss what support the reviewee needs – including from the manager – to achieve their performance objectives.

Past development

This part of the conversation can also begin by inviting the reviewee to reflect on how they have developed over the past 12 months. Prompt questions might be:

- What were your development objectives for the past year? (Assuming these existed!)
- In terms of your skills, knowledge and confidence, what did you learn over the past 12 months?
- Which experiences contributed to your learning?
- What were you hoping to learn last year that didn't happen?

Again, the manager might add their own observations on how they think the reviewee has progressed, particularly if they think that they are understating how they have grown.

Future development

While this part of the conversation might focus on the next 12 months, it may be important to set the discussion in the context of the reviewee's career aspirations. In some organisations, the performance and development review process feeds into a wider talent management and succession planning process. It could be that the individual's career goals mean that they may leave their current organisation – the nature of the relationship between the manager and the individual will influence how openly this can be discussed (or even acknowledged).

Here are some questions to structure this part of the process.

- What are your career aspirations? (An alternative phrasing might be something along the lines of, Where do you see yourself in five years' time?)
- What skills, knowledge or experience do you wish to gain over the coming 12 months?
- What activities will facilitate this?
- What specific development goals do you wish to set yourself for the year ahead?
- What actions do these require?
- What support do you need, including from me as your manager?

Once again, the manager may have relevant ideas on where the individual could usefully develop, and can share these having first listened to the reviewee's thoughts on their development.

I noted at the start of this chapter the danger that an annual review produces paperwork that doesn't get looked at until the next round 12 months later. It is much more useful if the review is seen as a live process, with follow-up conversations on both performance goals and development plans throughout the year. I've noted at various points in the book that the conversation that a manager has – or doesn't have – with the people who work for them are crucial in defining the nature of the relationship. Taking care to prioritise regular review conversations throughout the year can be invaluable.

In some organisations the annual review process is a central contributor to decisions on pay increases or monetary bonuses. As noted earlier, it may also feed into discussions on succession planning. I don't want to appear naïve here – how well someone performs is crucial to the rewards they receive and to their progression in their career. However, a potential downside of this is that it may well limit the honesty with which either party engages in the review conversation.

RESOURCE AND VIDEO

Performance Management: An Introduction (CIPD, 2024): www.cipd.org/en/knowledge/factsheets/performance-factsheet/

The website of the Chartered Institute of Personnel and Development includes a factsheet and a two-minute video in which Jonny Gifford discusses current best practice in performance management. One of the points he makes in the video is that enhancing your strengths may well be a more effective approach to development than correcting weaknesses.

Chapter 17: Q

QUESTIONING AND PLAYING BACK

In Chapter 6 I noted four skills that are invaluable in conversations that get to the heart of the matter – listening, questioning, playing back and voicing your views clearly. In this chapter I'll explore further effective questioning and the value of playing back what others have said. I look at listening in Chapter 41 and at voicing in the final chapter of the book when I discuss assertiveness.

Questioning

The ability to ask good questions is a key skill in finding out the views of others, which in turn can provide a valuable basis for making decisions, generating ideas, influencing and negotiating.

A useful distinction is between closed and open questions. A closed question can be answered *yes* or *no*, or with a one-word answer. An open question, on the other hand, invites a fuller response, which is likely to prompt more thinking in the other person and to generate more information. Here is a simple illustration, which also illustrates that it is easy to turn a closed question into an open one.

- Closed: *Are you finding this book useful?*
- Open: *What are you finding useful in this book?*

Closed questions usually begin with a verb – '*Are you...?*', '*Should you...?*', '*Can you...?*', etc. Open questions begin with words like

What?, *How?*, *In what way?*, etc. An invitation such as *'Say a bit more about…'* is effectively an open question.

There are, of course, times when you do want a *yes* or *no* answer, and a closed question is appropriate. For example, you might end a conversation by asking a question such as *'Will you be able to finish the report by Friday lunchtime?'*

One type of open question that is sometimes problematic is a question that begins with *Why?* Asking *'Why did you do that?'* can come across as very challenging, and might put the other person on the defensive, feeling that they need to justify themselves. I find it useful to soften a *Why?* question. Here are two examples. The first is backward-looking, and expressed with a degree of tentativeness. The second is forward-looking.

- I'm wondering what led you to do that?
- What do you think this will achieve?

On the other hand, a *Why?* question can be helpful in exploring an issue. There is a method known at the 5 Whys Technique. Having identified and defined a problem, you simply ask a *Why?* question five times, building on each answer as you seek to identify the root cause of the problem.

Another type of question which is problematic is a leading question – that is, one which already contains the answer or at least a suggested answer. I think it is cleaner, when you have a suggestion to make, simply to make the suggestion rather than dress it up as a question. Here is an illustration, with a cleaner alternative:

- Do you think it would be a good idea to do X?
- I think it might be a good idea to do X. What do you think?

A word that I like to use to describe a good question is *crisp*. I find that taking a little time to formulate a short, open question is very helpful, and much better than asking long or multiple questions. It's often easy to ask a powerful question in just half a dozen words. For example:

- What are we trying to achieve?
- How might you do this?
- What concerns do you have?

If you don't take a little time to formulate your question, you run the risk of asking long, complicated questions or perhaps a series of questions – leaving the other person confused about what exactly you are asking.

I notice too that people sometimes ask a question and then add their own thoughts, sometimes to justify their question. Radio and TV interviewers often do this. If you think that you need to explain your thinking when asking a question, I recommend that you do this first and then close with the question. Consider these two formulations.

- What do you think we should do? There are advantages in option A, but there are also downsides. And plan B has costs and benefits too. On balance, I'm inclined to pursue A.
- We have two options, A and B, and there are advantages and disadvantages to both. I'm inclined to pursue A. What do you think we should do?

Playing back

I find that playing back to someone what they've been saying is a simple yet powerful way to do a number of things. It lets me check my understanding, giving the other person the opportunity to correct any misunderstanding on my part. Playing back an empathic and non-judgemental understanding of their view is a great way to demonstrate a genuine interest in the other person. And this in turn helps to build a relationship of rapport between us.

There are three ways in which I play back.

1. First, I might *summarise* what the other person has been saying. This is usually about an extended piece of conversation.
2. Second, I might *paraphrase* what they say, turning their words into my own. However, there is a risk that, in modifying their language, my paraphrase isn't accurate.
3. To avoid distorting what they mean, the third way in which I play back is to repeat their exact words. I call this *reflecting back.* There are times when the precise wording used by someone is especially significant. I might ask them to say a bit more about [*their exact words*]. Or I might simply repeat [*their words*] with an inquisitive tone.

Playing back in these ways is valuable both in one-to-one conversations and in meetings. Summarising the key points that have been made by different people in a discussion can be really useful. It can also help to structure and manage the conversation, closing one part and moving on to the next. It can be used very effectively in a negotiation, acknowledging the position and priorities of the other party – which doesn't mean that you agree with them!

I often find, particularly in a one-to-one conversation, that the combination of a summary followed by a crisp question is a very effective way of managing a session. It can also be an acceptable way of interrupting someone who is going on at length or of closing a discussion that's begun to ramble. I sometimes call this *interrupting myself* – I'll acknowledge what has been said and then move the conversation on. This feels less rude than simply cutting someone off.

> **VIDEO**
>
> The Power of Effective Questioning (Litmos Heroes, 2014): www.youtube.com/watch?v=1dO0dO__wmE
>
> This six-minute video explores a number of ideas around questioning.

Chapter 18: R
MANAGEMENT AS A RELATIONSHIP

One of the fundamental ideas that underlie this book is that the relationship between you as a manager and the people who work for you is vitally important. The relationship that you seek to create with your people reflects how you see your role as a manager, and also how you view the people in your team.

Concern for task and concern for people

Robert Blake and Jane Mouton (1964) developed a simple but powerful framework which they called the *managerial grid*. As a manager who – by definition – seeks to achieve things through other people, you need to balance concern for the task and concern for the people involved. Figure 18.1 illustrates five approaches.

Many managers concentrate exclusively on ensuring that the task is completed, sometimes in a cold, unfeeling way. This may gain compliance, but is unlikely to get the full commitment of the people. And there are other managers whose priority seems to be making sure everyone in the team is happy – this is likely to be at the expense of delivering what's needed for the organisation.

There isn't necessarily a trade-off between addressing the needs of the task and the needs of the people. A successful team leader realises that the task is achieved through the efforts of the people involved, and will spend time addressing both sets of needs.

Figure 18.1 The managerial grid: concern for task and concern for people

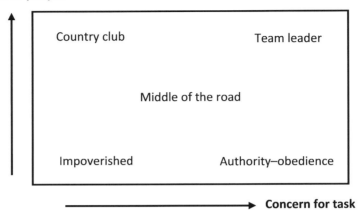

Command and control – or coaching

A manager who focuses primarily on achieving the task (characterised as Authority–obedience in Figure 18.1) may well have a *command and control* view of their role. They set objectives for their people, communicate these clearly, monitor how successfully the objectives are being met and make adjustments if necessary. The objectives for the team and its individual members may be based on higher-level objectives which cascade down the organisation. *Management by objectives* is a rational, clear approach to achieving results, and is widely used in many organisations.

The term *command and control* may sound negative. Putting this in more neutral language, it is about giving instructions, ensuring that these instructions are carried out and restricting the scope for discretion and judgement. There are many situations in which this is appropriate. In setting and monitoring objectives, the manager is *telling* people what to do. And often the people being managed in this way expect this at least as much as those in authority.

In Chapter 3 I explored the idea of a coaching dance where a manager moves skilfully between *telling* people what to do and *asking* them for their ideas. You might describe this as a *coaching* approach to management rather than *command and control*. A coaching approach calls for a genuine belief in the potential of people, a trust that others will perform and a willingness to let go when appropriate. A coaching approach seeks to tap into the potential and creativity of others, which can be highly motivating for them. This can free the manager up to tackle more strategic issues. Moreover, giving people the opportunity to take on more responsibility will enhance their capability, their confidence and their sense of self. A coaching approach is a great way of developing your people.

A manager who adopts a command and control approach will have very different conversations with those who work for them, and will create very different relationships, than someone who uses a coaching approach as a key part of how they carry out their role.

Parent, Adult and Child ego states

In Chapter 2 I looked at the ideas of ego states and transactions from the field of Transactional Analysis (TA). In that chapter I wrote:

> *In thinking about transactions, or more generally relationships, in a work context, a common pattern of interaction is that a manager operates from a Critical Parent ego state, which prompts an Adapted Child response from someone who reports to them. Indeed, the whole culture of a department or an organisation might be characterised by such Parent–Child interactions between managers and reports. This is likely to be an environment of command and control.*

When the culture of an organisation is characterised by this type of interaction between management and staff, it is very difficult for an individual manager to operate differently. For example, some organisations are necessarily bureaucratic. There will inevitably and appropriately be limits on how far you can empower people in such an organisation.

It can also be the case that the origin of a Parent–Child pattern of transactions lies with a member of staff who is unwilling to take appropriate responsibility for performing their role. As I noted in Chapter 2, you cannot make someone operate from their Adult state – you can only invite them to.

In Chapter 2 I also wrote this paragraph, which might reflect – in terms of Blake and Mouton's model – a Country club or an Impoverished approach to management:

> *A less common pattern of transactions within a team is that the manager operates from Nurturing Parent, seeking to overprotect someone or failing to address problematic behaviour or poor performance. This again runs the risk of stimulating an Adapted Child response where a report doesn't take proper accountability for their contributions.*

A coaching approach to managing people can be viewed as an attempt to create an Adult–Adult relationship. This pattern of interacting is generally the most productive. It's also likely to be more enjoyable and satisfying for both parties.

Images of manager

In Chapter 15 I explored different images of an organisation. The most common image or metaphor regards an organisation as a *machine*, made up of interlocking parts which fit together in a hierarchical structure. An equivalent metaphor for a manager is the manager as a *controller* whose role is to plan, organise, monitor and control. Like the machine metaphor, the control metaphor works well when the environment is stable and the human parts are compliant. It is limiting, however, in times of change or complexity.

Just as there are different metaphors for an organisation, so too there are different metaphors for a manager. In the next chapter

I'll look at servant leadership, which sees the role of a manager as being to serve others, including the people who work for them. All metaphors are partial, neither true nor false. What matters is whether a metaphor yields useful insights. You might like to spend a few minutes thinking of ideas or actions that the following metaphors for a manager suggest:

- controller;
- conductor;
- captain;
- coach;
- gardener;
- architect;
- shepherd;
- navigator;
- translator;
- servant.

Reflecting on how you yourself manage people, which of these metaphors best describe your approach? And which metaphors suggest ways in which you might usefully flex your style?

> **RESOURCE AND VIDEO**
>
> Putting the Human Back Into Human Resources (Mary Schaefer, 2015): www.linkedin.com/pulse/putting-human-back-resources-mary-schaefer-mhrm-shrm-cp/
>
> In this post and ten-minute TED talk Mary Schaefer discusses how each of us wants to be appreciated, to belong and to make a meaningful contribution at work.

Reference

Blake, R and Mouton, J (1964) *The Managerial Grid*. Houston: Gulf.

Chapter 19: S

SERVANT LEADERSHIP

At the end of the previous chapter I noted a number of metaphors for a manager, including the idea of the manager as servant. The term *servant leadership* was first coined in 1970 by Robert Greenleaf in an essay entitled 'The Servant as Leader'. He wrote:

> *Becoming a servant-leader begins with the natural feeling that one wants to serve, to serve first. Then conscious choice brings one to aspire to lead. That person is sharply different from one who is leader first ...*

> *The difference manifests itself in the care taken by the servant first to make sure that other people's highest priority needs are being served. The best test, and most difficult to administer, is: Do those served grow as persons? Do they, while being served, become healthier, wiser, freer, more autonomous, more likely themselves to become servants? And what is the effect on the least privileged in society; will they benefit, or, at least, not be further deprived?*
>
> (in Spears, 1998)

A simple illustration of servant leadership is seen in an inverted organisation chart which puts the people who deal with the organisation's customers, clients, patients or students, etc. at the top of the chart, those who manage the customer-facing staff below, and senior management at the bottom of the chart supporting everyone else.

In his introduction to Joe Jaworski's book, *Synchronicity* (1998), Peter Senge writes:

> *For Greenleaf, being a leader has to do with the relationship between the leader and the led. Only when the choice to serve undergirds the moral formation of leaders does the hierarchical power that separates the leader and those led not corrupt. Hierarchies are not inherently bad, despite the bad press they receive today. The potential of hierarchy to corrupt would be dissolved, according to Greenleaf, if leaders chose to serve those they led – if they saw their job, their fundamental reason for being, as true service.*

Probably the best-known servant leader in public life in recent times was Nelson Mandela. He had a clear vision that was essentially in the service of others. And he was able to engage others effectively in the pursuit of that vision.

The servant leader metaphor may seem naïve and impractical to someone whose underlying metaphor of leadership is about command and control. Some managers with a strong need to control others find it very difficult to trust their people. The opposite of control within an organisation is not necessarily lack of control. In many ways, the opposite of control is trust.

In an interview with Larry Spears some months after the 9/11 tragedy of 2002, Margaret Wheatley reflects on what to do when you can't control events. She says that:

> *The only way to lead when you don't have control is you lead through the power of your relationships. You can deal with the unknown only if you have enormous levels of trust, and if you're working together and bringing out the best in people. I don't know of any other model that can work in the world right now except servant-leadership.*
>
> (Wheatley, 2002)

Characteristics of a servant leader

On his website Larry Spears (2018) discusses ten characteristics of a servant leader which he originally extracted from Robert Greenleaf's writings. These are as follows.

1. **Listening** intently to others, hearing what is being said and unsaid, and clarifying the will of a group. It also includes listening to one's own inner voice.
2. **Empathy.** Understanding, accepting and recognising people for their special and unique spirits.
3. **Healing.** Servant leadership has the potential for helping others to recover from emotional hurt or broken spirit. It can also help to heal one's self and one's relationships with others.
4. **Awareness**, including self-awareness, which helps to view issues, particularly those involving ethics, power and values, from a more integrated, holistic position.
5. **Persuasion.** The ability to persuade and convince others distinguishes servant leadership from a traditional authoritarian, coercive approach.
6. **Conceptualisation.** The ability to balance attention to day-to-day operational matters with the ability to think more broadly and conceptually – to *'dream great dreams'* (Spears, 2018).
7. **Foresight.** The ability to learn from the past, to appreciate the reality of the present and to anticipate the future consequences of a decision. It may require intuition.
8. **Stewardship.** Holding things in trust for others and for the greater good of society.
9. **Commitment to the growth of people.** Appreciating the intrinsic value of people, and nurturing their personal and professional development.
10. **Building community.** Recognising that many people today work in large institutions, a servant leader seeks to create true community among those who work in their organisation.

Servant leadership and a coaching approach to management

Servant leadership is about supporting people, seeking to bring out the best in them, trusting them, and dispensing with the illusion of control. One way of translating servant leadership into practice within an organisation is through a coaching approach to management and to relationships. Listening in order to understand people, and asking questions to help them clarify what matters to them and what they need to do to succeed, are ways to coach others, to lead others and to serve others. Coaching, like servant leadership, is far more than some tools in the managerial toolkit. At its best, coaching, like servant leadership, is a way of *being* as well as a way of managing.

In her interview with Larry Spears mentioned earlier, Margaret Wheatley also says:

> *But what I find in servant-leadership that I still find missing in the world is this fundamental respect for what it means to be human. And I think that right now the greatest need is to have faith in people. That is the single most courageous act of a leader. Give people resources, give them a sense of direction, give them a sense of their own power and just have tremendous faith that they'll figure it out.*
>
> (Wheatley, 2002)

You might like to take a few minutes to reflect upon the extent to which you see your own role as a manager as being to serve the people whom you lead and the other stakeholders in your work. If you were to serve others more fully in your role, what might you do differently?

> **VIDEO**
>
> Ken Blanchard – Servant Leadership (London Business Forum, 2017): www.youtube.com/watch?v=ctZHSa4Qhd4
>
> In this three-minute video, Ken Blanchard, co-author of *The One Minute Manager*, talks about servant leadership and some related ideas.

References

Greenleaf, R (1998) *The Power of Servant Leadership* (edited by L Spears). San Francisco: Berrett-Koehler.

Jaworski, J (1998) *Synchronicity*. San Francsico: Berrett-Koehler.

Spears, L (ed) (1998) *Insights on Leadership*. New York: John Wiley.

Spears, L (2018) Ten Characteristics of a Servant-Leader. [online] Available at: www.spearscenter.org/46-uncategorised/136-ten-characteristics-of-servant-leadership (accessed 27 February 2024).

Wheatley, M (2002) The Servant-Leader: From Hero to Host. [online] Available at: www.margaretwheatley.com/articles/herotohost.html (accessed 27 February 2024).

Chapter 20: T
MANAGING A TEAM

Just because a group of people report to the same person, or sit in the same office, it doesn't follow that they are a team. When I worked in the gas pipeline company Transco, I once facilitated an away day for the people who were the immediate reports of the director of support services. There was the HR manager and the purchasing manager, the head of procurement, the chief lawyer and a few others. While they did need at times to discuss some strategic issues facing the company, they essentially were responsible for different parts of the operation. Although they all had the same boss, they didn't need to be a team – or to go on a team-building day!

So, what distinguishes a team from a group of people? In their book *The Wisdom of Teams* Jon Katzenbach and Douglas Smith offer a very useful definition of a team:

> *A team is a small number of people with complementary skills committed to a common purpose, performance goals and ways of working together for which they hold themselves mutually accountable.*
>
> (Katzenbach and Smith, 1994)

All of the phrases in the definition have been carefully chosen, and it is worth studying them in some detail.

Small number of people

In their research, Katzenbach and Smith found that most teams had ten or less members. When groups were larger than that, it was rare for them to be a genuine team. I once had the privilege of working with David Whitaker to deliver coaching skills programmes for Transco managers. David was the coach of the British men's hockey team which won the gold medal at the Seoul Olympics in 1988. He explained how he oversaw a number of teams within the overall set-up. On the pitch, there was the defence, the midfield and the attack. Behind the scenes there were the coaching staff, the physios and the medics, for example. Each of these needed to work as a team, and David had to co-ordinate the activities of all of them. In a similar way, Transco's director of support services needed to oversee the work of the various departments reporting to him.

Complementary skills

As the example of a hockey team shows, people with diverse skills are needed to play specialist roles in different positions. The leader of the team needs to recruit wisely to create an effective balance. As a manager in an organisation, you may inherit an existing group without the luxury of recruiting exactly whom you need – this requires you to develop individuals to provide all of the various competences needed.

Common purpose

I think this is a crucial element. An effective team shares a clear understanding of the reason why they are there. This might be to play their part in the delivery of a wider strategy set by the organisation in which they sit. Or they might be an independent organisation that has more freedom to create their purpose. This might be aspirational but needs to be grounded in reality. For example, if you are the manager of the local pub football team, you might wish to win a trophy next season – but it's never going to be the Champions League!

Performance goals

The common purpose of the team needs to be translated into more detailed performance goals, with appropriate time frames and metrics. In some organisations these are expressed as Key Performance Indicators (KPIs) – specific targets which capture financial, customer-focused or operational objectives. As a manager, you need to monitor the achievement of these KPIs.

Ways of working together

It takes time for a group to become a team. One reason for this is that it requires time to discuss and agree how the members of the group wish to work together. In September each year, around 120 students join the full-time MBA at Warwick Business School. They will spend the first term working in syndicates of seven or eight people. A key challenge for each syndicate is to establish agreement on practical things (for example, timekeeping, making decisions and taking roles such as scribe, timekeeper or chair) and on more difficult matters (for example, handling disagreement or different aspirations effectively). All of this has the added challenge that they are a group of peers without a designated leader. Some syndicates develop well over the course of the term – and some get stuck in polite avoidance or damaging conflict.

Mutually accountable

This is a key and essential feature of a genuine team. Members take responsibility to support one another. For example, if one of the team is having a bad day, others step forward to help without waiting for the boss to tell them. It's a good example of an issue where, as the manager, you need to facilitate the development of mutual accountability – and then let go and trust the individuals to enact it.

Committed

This sits along with mutual accountability. Commitment is more than agreement. When things get tough, someone who is committed will step up and do what's required. Someone who has agreed may or may not step forward. And someone who has merely complied is even less likely to take responsibility for action when things are difficult.

Models of team development

Probably the best know model of team development is Bruce Tuckman's *Forming, Storming, Norming, Performing* model. In my view, groups don't necessarily go through these stages. I think that a more useful model is that set out by John Whitmore in his book *Coaching for Performance* (2002). He suggests that groups go through these three stages:

1. inclusion;
2. assertion;
3. co-operation.

In the *Inclusion* stage, people are gauging to what extent they are included in the group. They may be feeling insecure, and possibly asking themselves if they want to be in this group. Some people will deal with their anxiety about acceptance or rejection by being quiet or tentative, while others may compensate by being vocal or forceful.

In the *Assertion* stage, people who feel included begin to assert themselves in order to stake a claim for their territory within the group and their place in the pecking order. There may be power struggles and lots of competition within the group. This can make the group productive – you might imagine, for example, a group of sales people striving to deliver the best individual sales figures each month. Many groups do not advance beyond the Assertion stage. (As I shall discuss in the final chapter, it's useful to distinguish between a one-way version of basic assertiveness and a two-way version of genuine assertiveness. The Assertion stage of Whitmore's model is about basic assertiveness.)

In the *Co-operation* stage, people who feel established begin to support each other and to trust each other. There is a lot of commitment to the team, patience and understanding of each other, and humour and enthusiasm. There is also a willingness to challenge ideas, debate issues constructively and resolve conflict. The team is aligned well towards the achievement of its goals.

Note that it is entirely possible that a team will slip backwards at times to earlier stages of development.

You might like to reflect upon the group that you manage (or are a member of). To what extent is the group genuinely a team? Which individuals are in the Inclusion, Assertion or Co-operation stages?

> **VIDEOS**
>
> John Whitmore's Team Development Model (Mike Clayton, 2020): www.youtube.com/watch?v=VxPzQMseW7E
>
> In this six-minute video Mike Clayton discusses John Whitmore's model of team development.
>
> Katzenbach and Smith: The Wisdom of Teams (Mike Clayton, 2021): www.youtube.com/watch?v=jAKsyFti90M
>
> In this 11-minute video Mike Clayton discusses the key ideas in Katzenbach and Smith's book *The Wisdom of Teams*, including their model of the stages of development of a team:
>
> - working group;
> - pseudo team;
> - potential team;
> - real team;
> - high-performance team.

References

Katzenbach, J and Smith, D (1994) *The Wisdom of Teams*. New York: Harper.

Tuckman, B (1965) Developmental Sequence in Small Groups. *Psychological Bulletin*, 63(6): 384–99.

Whitmore, J (2002) *Coaching for Performance*. London: Nicholas Brealey.

Chapter 21: U

UN SUSTAINABLE DEVELOPMENT GOALS

In the LeadershipPlus module for full-time MBA students at Warwick Business School, we include a two-day workshop on ethics and sustainability. We believe that these are important topics that tomorrow's managers and leaders must embrace. I look at ethics in the next chapter, and in this chapter I'll explore some ideas about sustainability. Some years ago, it seemed that talking about sustainability was inviting our students to explore new ground – but for the past few years it's felt that all of our students are well aware of the sustainability challenges facing the world.

In 2015 the United Nations adopted 17 Sustainable Development Goals (SDGs) *'as a universal call to action to end poverty, protect the planet, and ensure that by 2030 all people enjoy peace and prosperity'* (UNDP, nd). These goals recognise that *'development must balance social, economic and environmental sustainability'* (UNDP, nd) and are as follows.

1. No poverty.
2. Zero hunger.
3. Good health and well-being.
4. Quality education.
5. Gender equality.
6. Clean water and sanitation.
7. Affordable and clean energy.
8. Decent work and economic growth.
9. Industry, innovation, and infrastructure.

10. Reduced inequality.
11. Sustainable cities and communities.
12. Responsible consumption and production.
13. Climate action.
14. Life below water.
15. Life on land.
16. Peace, justice, and strong institutions.
17. Partnerships to achieve the goal.

Challenges such as global warming or huge reductions in biodiversity are genuinely wicked problems facing the world. There are no easy solutions. Moreover, there seems to be a lack of political leadership to effectively address them. It's beyond the scope of this book to explore this. But let's discuss sustainability at the level of organisations.

Organisational level

It is usual today for companies to pursue Environmental, Social and Governance (ESG) objectives alongside purely financial goals. The claims made by many firms are simply *greenwashing* – that is, less than honest communications to persuade customers that their products are environmentally friendly and produced through ethical supply chains. However, there are organisations which seem to be committed to the genuine pursuit of ESG objectives.

A good example of a firm which seems honestly to pursue an integrated ESG agenda successfully is the Anglo-Dutch consumer goods company Unilever. Paul Polman, CEO between 2009 and 2019, implemented a vision reduce the company's environmental footprint, increase its social impact, provide a great workplace for employees and generate excellent financial returns to shareholders. The recent book which he co-authored, *Net Positive*, has the subtitle *How Courageous Companies Thrive by Giving More Than They Take*. In it he writes:

> All *businesses now face a profound choice: continue pursuing the shareholder-first model that forces shortsighted decisions, hurts business, and endangers our collective well-being ... or build businesses that grow and prosper over the long haul by serving the world – that is, by giving more than they take.*
>
> (Polman and Winston, 2022, emphasis in original)

As the quote suggests, leaders of companies have a choice as to whether to take a *shareholder* view or a wider *stakeholder* perspective. The shareholder view, which is widespread in reality, was expressed very clearly in the works of the economist Milton Friedman. He was an important influence on the thinking and policies of Margaret Thatcher and Ronald Reagan. In his book *Capitalism and Freedom,* he wrote:

> *There is one and only one social responsibility of business – to use its resources and engage in activities designed to increase its profits so long as it stays within the rules of the game, which is to say, engages in open and free competition without deception or fraud.*
>
> (Friedman, 1962)

The stakeholder perspective, on the other hand, is summarised in John Elkington's idea of the *triple bottom line* – people, planet and profits. In other words, firms should measure the social and environmental impact of their operations as well as the bottom line of their financial performance. The idea is developed in more detail by Carol Sandford (2011) in a framework which she calls the Pentad. This might be regarded as a *quintuple bottom line*.

Figure 21.1 The Pentad

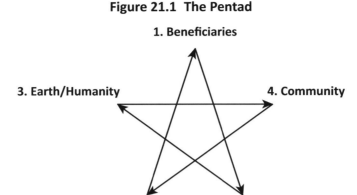

Figure 21.1 describes the Pentad in a way which applies to not-for-profit organisations as well as businesses. The numbering of the five stakeholders is significant.

The people who are the beneficiaries of the organisation's efforts (such as customers, consumers, residents or patients) come first. Satisfying their needs is the foundation of the operations. Second come the co-creators (such as employees, contractors, suppliers and volunteers) who contribute to the creation of the products or services that are offered. Earth/humanity is the third point, reflecting the need for the organisation to think about its long-term relationship to the planet and its people. The fourth group are the communities which are impacted by operations, including those of suppliers and the places where it recycles, stores or dumps its waste. The final stakeholder group are the investors or funders, without whom the organisation could not operate.

It's important to think about the five sets of stakeholders as an interlocking system so that the organisation acts in a responsible manner and in an integrated way to balance the needs of its different constituencies. Sandford (2011) writes:

> *The systemic approach described in this book is designed to support leadership or management that wants to embed*

responsibility into its way of doing business. It is a way of working that can be applied to any scale or type of business.

For an organisation to play its part in meeting the enormous challenges of the UN's 17 Sustainable Development Goals, it seems to me that it needs to adopt a systemic approach such as that offered by the Pentad framework. I'm conscious that it's infinitely easier to write that sentence than to translate it into practice!

> **RESOURCE AND VIDEO**
>
> Should Companies Lead on Sustainability? (Yale Insights, 2017): https://insights.som.yale.edu/insights/should-companies-lead-on-sustainability
>
> In this text and eight-minute video of an interview with Paul Polman, he discusses how Unilever sought to decouple the company's growth from its environmental impact. He goes on to discuss some of the challenges to business leaders in meeting the UN's Sustainable Development Goals.

References

Elkington, J (1998) Accounting for the Triple Bottom Line. *Measuring Business Excellence*, 2(3): 18–22.

Friedman, M (1962) *Capitalism and Freedom*. Chicago: Chicago University Press.

Polman, P and Winston, A (2022) *Net Positive: How Courageous Companies Thrive by Giving More Than They Take*. Boston: Harvard Business Review Press.

Sandford, C (2011) *The Responsible Business: Reimagining Sustainability and Success*. Edmonds: InterOctave.

UNDP (nd) What Are the Sustainable Development Goals? [online] Available at: www.undp.org/sustainable-development-goals (accessed 27 February 2024).

Chapter 22: V
VIRTUE ETHICS

I mentioned at the start of the previous chapter that we include a two-day workshop on the important topics of ethics and sustainability for the full-time MBA students at Warwick Business School. I explored sustainability in that chapter, and in this one I'll look at ethics.

Three schools of normative ethics

Normative ethics is a branch of philosophy which provides a framework for how we ought to behave in different situations, helping us to determine what is right and wrong, good and bad. It addresses the question *What should I do?* There are three main approaches to normative ethics, each with strengths and weaknesses. Let's look at these in turn.

1. Consequentialism

This takes the view that the correct thing to do depends upon the consequences of human actions and not on the actions themselves. The ethically correct choice is the one that maximises the overall consequences. These might be to spread happiness, or to relieve suffering, or to create freedom, or to promote the survival of the species, for example. It takes the view that *the end justifies the means*.

The best-known form of consequentialism is utilitarianism. Utilitarianism's desired outcome is the greatest amount of good possible. It may be summed up in the guideline that the right thing to do is that which yields the *greatest good for the greatest number of people*.

One of the problems in a consequentialist approach is that often we don't know all of the consequences of our actions. Moreover, it may be difficult or impossible to define, let alone measure, utility. For example, how do you put a price on human life or dignity? Also, how do you add up the costs and benefits to different people when there are winners and losers from a decision?

2. Deontology

A second approach is deontology, from the Greek word *deon* which means *duty*. The right thing to do in any situation is simply to follow the rules and do your duty. This seems simple and straightforward. Unlike consequentialism, it doesn't require assessing the outcomes of a decision or weighing the costs and benefits of a choice. Ethical actions often follow universal moral laws, such as *It is wrong to kill. Don't steal. Never tell lies.*

Deontology is often associated with the philosopher Immanuel Kant. He stated his *categorical imperative* in this phrase: *'Act only according to that maxim whereby you can, at the same time, will that it should become a universal law.'*

However, there are problems in taking a deontological approach. Situations differ, and whether something is good or bad may depend on the context. Rigidly using specific rules about what is right in all circumstances might lead to doing the wrong thing. For example, if your four-year-old child asks you on Christmas Eve if Santa Claus really exists, you may decide that it's better to tell a white lie.

3. Virtue ethics

A third approach is known as virtue ethics. In this approach, an action is right if and only if it is an action that a virtuous person would do in the same circumstances. A virtuous person is someone who has a particularly good character. Someone who has developed virtuous habits is likely to make the right choice when faced with an ethical challenge.

The ancient Greek philosopher Aristotle wrote about the idea of the *golden mean*. Virtue is the golden mean between two vices, one of excess and the other of deficiency. For example, courage is a virtue – taken to excess it could become recklessness, while in deficiency it might be cowardice. A balanced approach would be to adjust to circumstances, guided by principles.

There are again problems in applying virtue ethics in practice. It may be difficult to identify exemplary role models to use as a guide. To behave virtuously requires deep self-knowledge and reflection. Moreover, judging situations can be difficult. And it may be hard to balance individual and collective interests.

The I-RIGHT framework

There are contexts in which a deontological approach is expected or even mandated – rules must be applied. I work in a university, and there are regulations that govern, for example, the marks required for different degree classifications. In my role as a senior tutor for half of the final year students at Warwick Business School, I frequently meet students who have encountered challenging circumstances which affected their ability to study and perform as well as they might in their assessments. Sadly, these mitigating circumstances often involve mental health issues. My colleagues in the administration team have to apply the rules consistently. I sometimes find myself arguing for a more balanced approach, showing some leniency or (I would argue) common sense. Without claiming to be virtuous, I think my approach is more along the lines of seeking a golden mean. I usually lose the argument!

As I've noted, there are problems in applying each of the three approaches. In his book *Ethicability* Roger Steare combines them in a framework which he calls RIGHT. He says:

Doing what's right doesn't always mean immediate success or even personal happiness, because life isn't a playground. How to do what's RIGHT is about thinking right, doing right, and leaving the world a better place.

(Steare, 2007)

I think it's useful to extend his model to become I-RIGHT. Faced with a decision on what is the right thing to do, begin by listing the options you have. Then, *for each individual option*, ask yourself these questions.

- Who is **involved**?   (build your stakeholder map)
- What are the **rules**?   (deontology)
- How do we act with **integrity?** (virtue)
- Who is this **good** for?   (consequentialism)
- Who could we **harm**?   (consequentialism)
- Will this stand the **test of time**? (consequentialism and virtue)

In his formulation, Steare (2007) expresses the final question as 'What's the **truth**?'

Looking over your answers to these questions will, hopefully, guide you on which option to choose. You might like to try this out on an issue with an ethical dimension that you currently face.

> **VIDEOS**
>
> Ethics Defined (Glossary) (McCombs School of Business, nd): https://ethicsunwrapped.utexas.edu/ethics-defined
>
> The series of short videos (each under two minutes) covers a range of approaches to ethics, including consequentialism and utilitarianism, deontology and virtue ethics.

Reference

Steare, R (2007) *Ethicability*. Tonbridge: Roger Steare Consulting Limited.

Chapter 23: W
WORK–LIFE BALANCE

A healthy work–life balance means different things to different people. You may be someone who really enjoys their job and feel that you are making a valuable contribution to your organisation, to other people or to society. You may be content to work long hours. You might agree with the words of Noel Coward that *'Work is much more fun than fun'*.

Or you might be someone who is doing a job simply as a way of paying the bills. Perhaps you don't enjoy your role, or maybe you don't get on with some of your colleagues, or possibly there are parts of your job that are boring or stressful.

In terms of your situation today, where would you place yourself on this spectrum?

I work to live  I live to work

There are many people who do not have the luxury of reducing their hours or choosing when to start and finish their working day. And there are others who take work home with them not because they want to but because they have to in order to complete all the tasks expected of them.

I'm writing these words in my office at home. It's 5.00 in the afternoon, and I'm wondering whether to continue writing for another hour or to go for a walk. Moreover, I've chosen to write this book. It's not part of my job. I realise that I'm immensely lucky to have such choices.

In her blog Allaya Cooks-Campbell offers this definition:

Healthy work–life balance refers to maintaining a harmonious relationship between your work and personal life. It involves consciously managing your time and energy to meet both professional and personal commitments while prioritizing self-care and well-being.

(Cooks-Campbell, 2023)

She goes on to list possible signs of an unhealthy work–life balance.

- *Constant overwork: Regularly working long hours, including weekends and holidays, without sufficient time for rest, relaxation, or personal activities.*

- *Neglected personal life: Sacrificing personal relationships, hobbies, and leisure activities due to excessive work demands.*

- *Burnout: Experiencing physical, mental, and emotional exhaustion due to chronic stress and work-related pressure.*

- *Lack of self-care: Failing to prioritise self-care activities, such as exercise, adequate sleep, and leisure time resulting in deteriorating physical and mental health.*

- *Strained relationships: Experiencing difficulties in maintaining healthy relationships with family, friends, and loved ones due to work-related commitments.*

(Cooks-Campbell, 2023)

Improving your work–life balance

In their article 'Work–Life Balance Is a Cycle, Not an Achievement', Iona Lupu and Mayra Ruiz-Castro (2021) write that achieving work–life balance '*is not a one-time fix, but rather, a cycle that we must engage in continuously as our circumstances and priorities evolve'*. They go on to discuss the five steps that make up the cycle:

1. *Pause and denormalize. Take a step back and ask yourself what's currently causing your stress or unhappiness.*

2. *Pay attention to your emotions. How do you feel about your situation? Being aware of your feelings may help you decide what changes you wish to make.*

3. *Reprioritize. What changes do you actually want to make? You might want to work less hours to spend more time with your family or friends, for example.*

4. *Consider your alternatives. Before jumping into solutions, consider what aspects of your work or life could be different to align better with your priorities.*

5. *Implement changes. Take action – this might be a 'public' change where you tell others what you're doing, or a 'private' change where you don't attempt to shift the expectations of your colleagues.*

(Lupu and Ruiz-Castro, 2021)

Here are a number of ideas on what you might do to make changes in how you balance work and non-work activities. I discussed some of these in Chapter 14. As you read through them, consider which would be most helpful for you personally.

- **Say *no* to some requests**. This may require you to behave assertively. And you need to live with the consequences.
- **Identify what is *important* and what is *urgent*.** Invest time in those activities which are important but not urgent. Planning ahead is likely to fall into this category.
- **Schedule your priorities**. I'm a fair-weather golfer. I book Friday mornings between April and September in my

Outlook calendar so that I can play nine holes of golf with my buddy, Phil. If something important comes up, I may need to cancel.
- **Work smarter, not harder.** Identify what jobs need to be done really well and which only need to be done satisfactorily (and which don't need doing at all). This is really hard if you're a perfectionist!
- **Play to your strengths.** This might be a major decision about what kind of work you do. Or it could be a more modest choice about which activities to do yourself and which to delegate or pass on to others (if you have that option).
- **When you stop, stop.** Some people use the journey home from work as an opportunity to unwind, leaving work behind. The advent of mobile phones, the internet, email and hybrid working all make it more difficult to keep your evenings free. Set your own rules (if you can) about how you want to use technology in your own time. Don't be afraid to unplug!
- **Take time off.** Spend time doing the non-work things that you enjoy – hobbies, time with friends, studying, for example. Book a holiday.
- **Relax, exercise, sleep well and be mindful.** What things help you to relax? What forms of exercise (if any) do you like to do? Some people love to go for a run – I hate this, so I don't do it! Some people get great value from mindfully paying attention to their breathing and the sensations in their body. These can all be ways to reduce stress.
- **Talk to people.** A constructive conversation with your manager or your colleagues may enable you to agree changes in how you organise your work and your time more effectively. Speaking with your partner or family might help to make useful changes and perhaps improve relationships.
- **Ask for help.** If you're really struggling and feeling very stressed, asking for help shows strength, not weakness.

> **VIDEO**
>
> How to Make Work–Life Balance Work (Nigel Marsh, 2010): www.ted.com/talks/nigel_marsh_how_to_make_work_life_balance_work?language=en
>
> In this ten-minute TED talk Nigel Marsh explores – with honesty and humour – how you can create a better and meaningful work–life balance.

References

Cooks-Campbell, A (2023) How to Have a Good Work–Life Balance. [online] Available at: www.betterup.com/blog/how-to-have-good-work-life-balance (accessed 27 February 2024).

Lupu, I and Ruiz-Castro, M (2021) Work–Life Balance Is a Cycle, Not an Achievement. *Harvard Business Review*, 29 January. [online] Available at: https://hbr.org/2021/01/work-life-balance-is-a-cycle-not-an-achievement (accessed 27 February 2024).

Chapter 24: X
THEORY X AND THEORY Y

Writing one hundred years ago, the French mining engineer and executive Henri Fayol set out a general theory of management or, in his term, business administration (from which the MBA degree takes its name). He was the first person to describe management as a top-down process based on planning and the organisation of people. He listed five functions which a manager needs to perform:

- plan;
- organise;
- co-ordinate;
- command;
- control.

A *command and control* approach to management is widespread in organisations today. It is an authoritative approach which emphasises the difference between managers and staff. The term refers back to Fayol, but does not do justice to the breadth of his approach that is summarised in the bullet points above. Taking a command and control approach means that you give people instructions and ensure that these instructions are carried out, with little or no scope for discretion and judgement. There are many situations – especially in a bureaucracy – where this is appropriate. As an illustration, if I go for a blood test, I hope that there are well-defined procedures that the hospital and laboratory staff carry out consistently.

In his book *The Human Side of Enterprise* Douglas McGregor (1960) discussed two styles of management – *Theory X* (authoritarian) and *Theory Y* (participative). Implicit within both of these are beliefs about people and what motivates them.

A Theory X approach to management assumes that people are inherently lazy, dislike work and seek to avoid responsibility. If this is your underlying mental model, you are unlikely to trust your staff and may feel that you need to micromanage them. Managing people from this perspective is indeed about command and control. If incentives and punishments are available to you, you are likely to use a mix of carrot and stick to ensure compliance with your instructions or orders.

In contrast, a Theory Y perspective assumes that people enjoy work and are talented, creative and able to motivate themselves. As a manager, if this is how you view your people, then your assumption is that they want to do a good job, and that this desire in itself is motivating. Hence you are likely to communicate openly, share decision-making and generate a climate of trust.

In Chapter 3 I contrasted a directive, telling approach to a non-directive coaching approach. A coaching approach sits well within a Theory Y mental model of the world. I discussed the idea of a coaching dance where, as a manager, you move skilfully between telling people what to do and asking them for their ideas.

While you might favour one view over the other, it is appropriate to use different approaches in different situations. For example, you might take a directive approach with a new starter who needs a lot of guidance, or in a crisis where it's vital to give clear directions. Alternatively, if you're fortunate enough to manage a team of highly skilled and well-motivated people, then a Theory Y approach will be far more effective.

Your style might also reflect the nature of the organisation you're working in. Theory X is likely to be more prevalent in an organisation where there are multiple levels in the hierarchy, with central control, tight objectives and little delegation of authority. Theory Y is more likely to be found in a smaller organisation with a flatter structure where there is a culture of empowerment and autonomy.

In his book, McGregor drew on the ideas of Abraham Maslow on what motivates people. In *Motivation and Personality* Maslow (1954) describes five levels of human needs. These are often depicted as a pyramid, as in Figure 24.1, although Maslow himself never represented them in this way. Maslow argued that needs at the lower levels have to be satisfied before individuals can attend to higher needs.

- **Physiological needs** – air, food and water, shelter, sleep, etc.
- **Safety needs** – health, security, employment, etc.
- **Belonging** – love, friendship, family.
- **Esteem** – achievement, status, respect of others, self-esteem.
- **Self-actualisation** – personal growth and fulfilment.

Figure 24.1 Maslow's hierarchy of needs

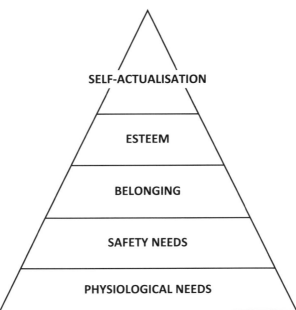

McGregor (1960) notes that *'management by direction and control'* fails to motivate because these are *'useless methods of motivating people whose physiological and safety needs are reasonably satisfied and whose social, egoistic, and self-fulfilment needs are predominant'*.

In an article entitled 'Beyond Theory Y', John Morse and Jay Lorsch (1970) build on McGregor's ideas. They put forward a contingency theory based on their investigation into what was happening in four different worksites. There needs to be an appropriate fit between task, structure and people.

They write that, *'the appropriate pattern of organization is contingent on the nature of the work to be done and on the particular needs of the people involved'* (Morse and Lorsch, 1970). They concluded that:

1. *Human beings bring varying patterns of needs and motives into the work organization, but one central need is to achieve a sense of competence.*

2. *The sense of competence motive, while it exists in all human beings, may be fulfilled in different ways by different people depending on how this need interacts with the strengths of the individuals' other needs – such as those for power, independence, structure, achievement, and affiliation.*

3. *Competence motivation is most likely to be fulfilled when there is a fit between task and organization.*

4. *Sense of competence continues to motivate even when a competence goal is achieved; once one goal is reached, a new, higher one is set.*

(Morse and Lorsch, 1970)

> **VIDEO**
>
> Douglas McGregor's Theory X and Theory Y (Organizational Communication Channel, 2016): www.youtube.com/watch?v=CXAzZRnJo2o
>
> This eight-minute video discusses further McGregor's Theory X and Theory Y, relating it again to Maslow's hierarchy of needs.

References

Fayol, H (1949) *General and Industrial Management*. London: Pitman and Sons.

Maslow, A (1954) *Motivation and Personality*. New York: Harper.

McGregor, D (1960) *The Human Side of Enterprise*. New York: McGraw-Hill.

Morse, J and Lorsch, J (1970) Beyond Theory Y. *Harvard Business Review*, May 1970. [online] Available at: https://hbr.org/1970/05/beyond-theory-y (accessed 27 February 2024).

Chapter 25: Y
GETTING TO YES

In their classic and bestselling book *Getting to Yes*, Roger Fisher and William Ury (1981) explain that each of us – like it or not – is a negotiator. We might be buying or selling a house, asking for a wage increase or agreeing a pay-out from an insurance company. We might be choosing with our family where to go on holiday this summer. Some people engage in commercial or trade union negotiations as part of their job. And others negotiate on the political stage, perhaps internationally.

Whatever the level, negotiation is a basic way of seeking to get what you want from others, involving some form of back-and-forth communication. People often adopt a *positional bargaining* strategy – they hold on to a fixed idea of what they want, and argue for their position. Some people take a *soft* approach, seeking to avoid conflict and making concessions easily. Others take a *hard* approach, viewing things as a battle of wills, which may damage relationships.

In *Getting to Yes*, Fisher and Ury (1981) set out an alternative approach to positional bargaining, which they call '*principled negotiation*'. This seeks to settle issues on their merits rather than by haggling over what each side will or won't do. It can be viewed as hard on the merits, soft on the people. It allows you to obtain what you are entitled to while still treating others fairly and without being taken advantage of. It is based on the following four fundamental principles.

1. Separate the people from the problem

Negotiators are people first. Their values or backgrounds may differ. There may be a clash of egos as people argue for their position. It can be easy for the relationship between the two parties to get mixed up with the substantive issues. When you separate the people from the problem, you seek to explore the issues without damaging the relationship between you and the other.

It's important to understand how the other party is viewing the situation – putting yourself in their shoes, as it were. *What really matters to them?* Note that understanding their viewpoint doesn't mean agreeing with it. But it helps you to get a clearer view of the essential problem that needs resolving.

2. Focus on interests, not positions

When you negotiate about interests, you seek to establish what you and the other party really want, not what both of you initially say that you want. Exploring what really matters to both parties may reveal that the underlying interests and needs of both are actually compatible, not mutually exclusive. It might actually be possible to find a solution which satisfies both parties' interests.

The starting point in identifying someone's interests is to explore why they hold the position that they do. There may be a number of interests which underlie their position. And it is essential also to explain your own interests clearly.

It's important too to look forward to creating a desirable solution, rather than holding a post-mortem on past events. Both parties need to keep their interests in mind but be open to different possibilities.

3. Invent options for mutual gain

It is necessary to seek to create solutions that allow both sides to win. It can be useful to brainstorm possibilities, being creative rather than critical. Rather than seeking to find a single answer, identify a variety of proposals. It helps to separate the invention of ideas from the evaluation of them. It's useful to begin evaluating the most promising proposals first – this might lead to some refinement too.

Focusing on shared interests can help to avoid a win–lose mentality. When interests differ, it can be helpful to identify what items will be of low cost to one party and high benefit to the other. Making an offer that will benefit the other party is likely to be more effective than issuing threats.

4. Insist on objective criteria

It is useful, if possible, to establish some objective criteria to assess whether an agreement is fair. Decisions that are based on reasonable standards will make it easier to reach an agreement that maintains a good relationship between the parties. For example, scientific findings, professional standards or legal precedents might help to define appropriate criteria.

There are three points to bear in mind when using objective criteria. First, the two parties should view this as a joint search for appropriate criteria on which to base agreements. Second, both parties need to be reasonable, to keep an open mind and be willing to reconsider their position when there is a good reason to do so. Third, while being reasonable, it's important not to give in to pressure or threats.

Handling conflict

I find the following short definition very useful: *Conflict is any form of disagreement, no matter how large or small*. In the framework shown in Figure 25.1, Kenneth Thomas and Ralph Kilmann

(1974) set out five ways in which you can address a disagreement or conflict. The five styles depend on whether you attempt to satisfy the needs of yourself or the needs of the other party.

1. If you seek to satisfy your own needs and disregard the needs of the other party, then the style is described as *competing*.
2. However, if you give priority to satisfying the needs of the other person and disregard your own needs, then this is described as *accommodating*.
3. If you make no attempt to satisfy ether your own or the other party's needs, then this is referred to as *avoiding*.
4. On the other hand, if you endeavour to meet both your own needs and the needs of the other person, this is called *collaborating*.
5. Finally, if you seek to meet some of your needs and some of the other party's – splitting the difference in some way, as it were – then this is called *compromising*.

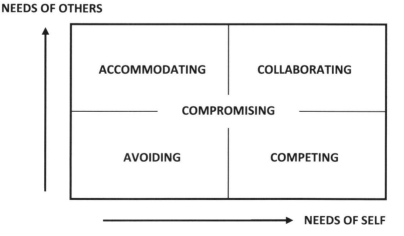

Figure 25.1 Five ways of handling conflict

Source: Based on Thomas and Kilmann, 1974

Fisher and Ury's idea of principled negotiation can be viewed as a collaborative attempt to find a win–win solution for both parties. There are, however, many situations where a win–win outcome isn't possible. Each of the five styles can be appropriate in different contexts.

The various styles of handling conflict are related to the idea of passive, assertive and aggressive behaviour. When you avoid a conflict or accommodate the needs of the other party, you may be acting passively. And when you compete to ensure that your own needs are met, you might be behaving aggressively. Being genuinely assertive – stating your views confidently and enabling the other party to state their views clearly – is required if you wish to find a collaborative outcome that is a win–win for both of you. Being genuinely assertive is essential in principled negotiation. I discuss assertiveness in the final chapter of the book.

> **VIDEO**
>
> Negotiation Principles: Getting to Yes (Productivity Game, 2019): www.youtube.com/watch?v=EKHg9H0G6go
>
> This eight-minute video is an excellent review of the key ideas in *Getting to Yes*.

References

Fisher, R and Ury, W (1981) *Getting to Yes*. Boston: Houghton Mifflin.

Thomas, K and Kilmann, R (1974) *Thomas–Kilmann Conflict Mode Instrument*. Mountain View: Xicom.

Chapter 26: Z
ZOOM AND HYBRID WORKING

Like many people, the Covid-19 pandemic meant that I had to adjust to working remotely during lockdowns and, more recently, in a hybrid way. I now go into Warwick Business School whenever I'm teaching and for a variety of other reasons. And I work from home several days a week, using Zoom or MS Teams to meet with individual students and to speak with colleagues. I also do most of my coaching and supervision work now via Teams, whereas before the first lockdown I did all of it face to face. When I do a mediation now, I usually have initial conversations via Teams with each individual and then facilitate the joint session face to face.

Hybrid working suits me well. I have a spare room that I can use as an office, I have good IT equipment and support, and my children are grown up (well, in years anyway!). I love the fact that when I switch off my laptop at the end of the afternoon, I don't have to think about what the traffic will be like on the drive home. I am an Introvert, and the absence of socialising with people at work doesn't bother me. I also had established good working relationships with colleagues before the pandemic struck. Interestingly, I have formed very good working relationships with a number of people over the past few years without ever meeting any of them face to face.

I realise, however, that many people struggled to work from home during lockdown and find that hybrid working doesn't suit them. It may be that the nature of their role doesn't fit well into a hybrid approach. They may not have the necessary facilities – including space and IT equipment – to work as effectively at home as they can at work. Some people miss hugely the ordinary day-to-day interactions with others. For some, the loss of connection with others has adversely affected their mental health and well-being.

In her article 'How to Do Hybrid Right', Lynda Gratton (2021) writes that, organisations will *'need to design hybrid work arrangements with individual human concerns in mind, not just institutional ones'*. She suggests that this requires thinking along the two axes of place and time outlined on Figure 26.1.

Figure 26.1 Work arrangements in place and time

	Constrained TIME	Unconstrained
PLACE Unconstrained	Anywhere, 9 to 5	Anywhere, any time
PLACE Constrained	Traditional office, 9 to 5	In the office, any time

Source: Based on Gratton, 2021

Gratton then explores four perspectives on the challenge of designing *'flexible working arrangements that can significantly boost productivity and employee satisfaction'* (2021).

1. Jobs and tasks

It is important to understand the key drivers of productivity in different roles. A receptionist, for example, has to be in the office during working hours. A strategic planner needs to focus, and can do this effectively either at home or in the office and at a time that suits their preferences. A team manager needs to co-ordinate the work of others, and this requires communication that often has to be synchronous. Time is critical, but place is less so if everyone has good IT facilities such as Zoom.

2. Employee preferences

In designing hybrid working arrangements, it is useful to take into account when possible the preferences of different individuals. For example, the domestic circumstances of some people mean that working from home suits them well, while others (perhaps people who have recently joined the organisation) benefit from spending time in the office with colleagues and their boss.

3. Projects and workflows

Creating new ways of working provides an opportunity to reassess how work gets done. It may be possible to bring in new technology. Or it might be valuable to step back and reimagine workflows – perhaps removing redundant procedures, reallocating responsibilities, automating processes or using space in novel ways.

4. Inclusion and fairness

Making changes to working arrangements can easily provoke feelings of unfairness and inequity. In turn, this may affect productivity, reduce collaboration, harm well-being and cause some staff to leave. It is important, therefore, to involve people in the design of new processes and to listen to their ideas and concerns.

Supporting mental health and well-being

Ensuring that people who are working remotely have the necessary technology, equipment and software is obviously essential. However, it is also vital to pay attention to the people and culture aspects of hybrid working.

An investigation by the Chartered Institute of Personnel and Development into lessons from the pandemic found that:

- *The most frequently mentioned benefit was increased wellbeing through avoiding the commute (46% of survey participants), followed by enhanced wellbeing because of greater flexibility of hours (39%).*

- *Reduced mental wellbeing of staff due to isolation was cited as a challenge by 44% of survey respondents.*

(CIPD, 2021)

Clearly, people react differently to working remotely. I don't think it's reasonable or realistic to expect a manager to guarantee the mental health and well-being of each person who works for them. The problems people face may be deep-rooted or caused by things that happen outside of work. However, I do think a manager needs to take into account the ways in which hybrid working arrangements may have an impact on individual well-being.

When someone is struggling, they are likely to exhibit signs such as a change in mood or behaviour or how they interact with others. They may withdraw, or show a lack of motivation or focus. They might appear tired or anxious. It is more difficult to spot these signs if you mainly engage with them online rather than face to face. You might not realise, for example, how isolated one of your staff is feeling.

Initiating a conversation with someone who's struggling is likely to be more difficult via Zoom or Teams than when you are with them in person. And having the conversation itself may well be more challenging too. It may be harder to pick up on non-verbal signals. However, the conversational skills of listening, questioning and playing back that I discussed in Chapter 6 remain the basis of an empathic conversation.

Working remotely also means that people don't engage in informal conversations with colleagues during breaks or at the start or finish of meetings on Zoom. And they are less likely to socialise with fellow workers. Some teams have been having informal interactions such as fun online quizzes. You might also set up a team away day or social activity to enable people to come together in person.

One way in which a manager can help to support others in a hybrid world is to act as a role model. Having clear working hours and not sending emails during evenings or weekends demonstrates that you yourself take seriously the need to have a good work–life balance.

Just as individuals may struggle due to lack of contact with others, so too teams may become less cohesive and effective when the members are together less often.

> **RESOURCE**
>
> Prioritising the Wellbeing of Your Workforce in a Hybrid Workplace (Nick Deligiannis, 2022): www.haystalentsolutions.com/-/prioritising-the-wellbeing-of-your-workforce-in-a-hybrid-workplace
>
> In this article, Nick Deligiannis considers how employers can support the mental health and well-being of their staff in a world of hybrid working.

References

CIPD (2021) Flexible Working: Lessons from the Pandemic. [online] Available at: www.cipd.org/globalassets/media/knowledge/knowledge-hub/reports/flexible-working-lessons-from-pandemic-report_tcm18-92644.pdf (accessed 27 February 2024).

Gratton, L (2021) How to Do Hybrid Right. *Harvard Business Review*, May–June. [online] Available at: https://hbr.org/2021/05/how-to-do-hybrid-right (accessed 27 February 2024).

And back again

Chapter 27: Z
ZOOKEEPING

In Chapter 15 where I explored two of Gareth Morgan's images for an organisation – the organisation as a machine and the organisation as a system – I noted that metaphors aren't true or false. Rather, what matters is whether or not a metaphor offers valuable insights. All metaphors are partial – they usefully illuminate some aspects of a situation but don't tell the whole story.

In Chapter 18 I noted a number of metaphors for the role of a manager, such as manager as controller, servant or shepherd. In this chapter I shall play with the idea of a manager as a zookeeper, hopefully generating some useful insights. This isn't commonly used as a metaphor for a manager, but I was struggling to find a suitable topic beginning with Z!

The website of Prospects, an organisation which helps students to find a suitable career, offers this definition:

> *Zookeepers are concerned with the welfare of animals kept in zoos, wildlife parks, aquariums and other animal attractions.*
>
> (Prospects, 2023)

The metaphor suggests the idea that a manager needs to be concerned with the welfare of their staff – I'll explore this in some detail in Chapter 30. And it indicates that there are different settings in which the work takes place – just as organisations operate in a variety of sectors. The metaphor implies that employees aren't the same species as the manager. I think the metaphor fails here, though I suspect that some managers do see themselves as vastly superior to their people!

The website of the government's National Careers Service states that the skills and knowledge needed for a zookeeper role are:

- *the ability to work well with others*
- *to be thorough and pay attention to detail*
- *excellent verbal communication skills*
- *the ability to use your initiative*
- *customer service skills*
- *knowledge of biology*
- *to be flexible and open to change*
- *patience and the ability to remain calm in stressful situations*
- *to be able to use a computer and the main software packages competently*

(National Careers Service, nd)

If you substitute *'knowledge of what makes people tick'* for *'knowledge of biology'*, you have a fairly good statement of the skills needed to manage people well!

Herding cats

A related metaphor lies in the phrase *'It's like herding cats'*. The task of managing academics is often described in this way. A quick look on the internet suggests that it might apply to lots of professions – such as lawyers or IT specialists. The role of a project manager can often feel like herding cats. An article on

ZOOKEEPING 141

the website of Praxis, a community resource for project and programme management, draws out this comparison.

> *Cats, of course, unlike herd animals prefer to go their own way much like humans in organisations. Although organisations want and need, as the name implies, to organise people toward common goals, particularly when changing the business, the reality is that most people have their own ideas, agendas and preferences. Which is why, when you have a business change programme or project – with many team members who have disparate skill sets and personalities – finding the right leader good enough to herd cats is of critical importance. This equally applies to both the key decision maker and programme/project manager roles respectively.*
>
> (Praxis, nd)

Owls, foxes, donkeys and sheep

While you might prefer to stay well away from the politics within your organisation, this isn't possible if you wish to promote the interests and projects which you feel are important. It might not be a good stance for your own survival too. In an article entitled 'Owl, Fox, Donkey or Sheep: Political Skills for Managers', Simon Baddeley and Kim James (1987) set out a framework of four approaches to handling the politics within an organisation.

As illustrated in Figure 27.1, the vertical axis considers how well someone is able to read the politics of a situation – how aware or unaware they are of what's going on around them – of things like how decisions are made, power and influence, overt and covert agendas, and culture.

The horizontal axis reflects whether the individual acts with integrity, on the one hand, or plays psychological games, on the other. This involves using the written rules about decision-making, procedures and negotiation and also the unwritten rules on things like lobbying, getting items onto agendas and the timing of when to put forward a proposal.

Figure 27.1 A model of political behaviour

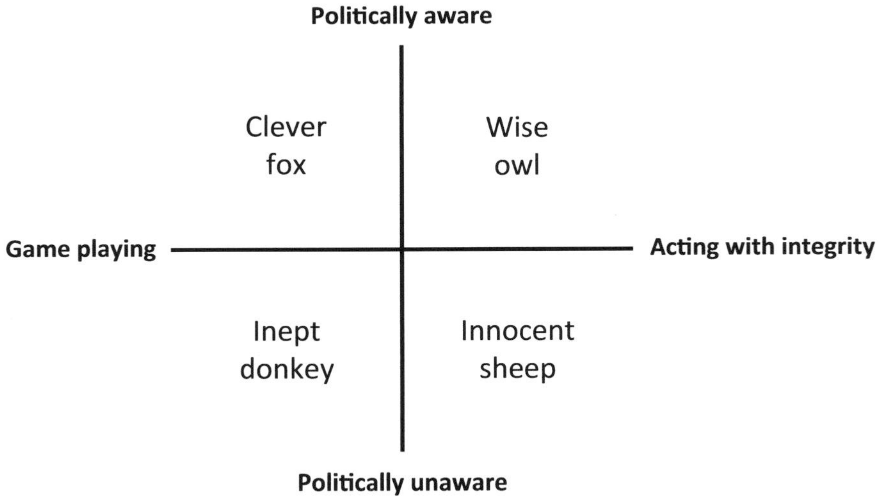

```
                    Politically aware
                          |
           Clever         |      Wise
           fox            |      owl
                          |
Game playing  ————————————+———————————— Acting with integrity
                          |
           Inept          |      Innocent
           donkey         |      sheep
                          |
                    Politically unaware
```

Source: Baddeley and James, 1987

The two dimensions can be combined to set out four ways in which people handle the politics of situations. These are summarised well in a blog by Paul Hutchinson:

Sheep are politically naïve but act in the group's interest, because they think it's the right thing for the organisation and the people. They are loyal and industrious but need to be led.

Donkeys, like sheep, are politically naïve – but the difference is that they act out of self-interest.

Owls are politically aware of the situation and the environment but ask how to do things for the overarching goal and the people. Loyal to the organisation, they possess integrity, and are respected by colleagues.

Foxes are also politically aware but act out of self-interest, putting themselves before others and even before the

organisation. But there's no doubt that they can make things happen, even though they are doing it for their benefit.
(Hutchinson, 2019)

You might like to reflect upon your own approach to the politics within your organisation. Which of the four styles do you typically take? Which do you rarely take? What might you do differently to be more effective or influential?

Think too of the people that you manage, your peers and those above you in the organisation chart. Who falls into each of the four categories? What might you do to manage or engage with them more successfully? And what might you do to capitalise on their skills and motivation?

Owls, foxes, donkeys and sheep in negotiations

In his book *Everything is Negotiable*, Gavin Kennedy (2008) draws on the idea of owls, foxes, donkeys and sheep to describe four approaches which people take to negotiations.

1. A sheep doesn't fight for their own interests, and accepts far too readily what other parties want. They seek to preserve harmony in relationships, and may withdraw if things get heated.
2. Someone who behaves like a donkey holds stubbornly to a fixed position. They may not think through what they might gain in negotiating constructively.
3. Owls are wise enough to realise the value of building trust and creating good relationships that may yield long-term benefits They are well aware of both opportunities and threats. In Chapter 25 I looked at the idea of principled negotiation, seeking to create win–win outcomes for all. An owl is best placed to pursue this.
4. A fox is well aware of what's happening, and is willing to battle aggressively to get what they want. In their arrogance, they fail to build trust or collaborative relationships.

> **RESOURCE AND VIDEO**
>
> How to Deal with Office Politics – Who Are Your Sheep, Donkeys, Foxes and Owls? (Thinking Focus, 2023): www.linkedin.com/pulse/how-deal-office-politics-who-your-sheep-donkeys-foxes/
>
> This link takes you to an article and a four-minute video that explores the different ways in which people address the challenges of politics within organisations.

References

Baddeley, S and James, K (1987) Owl, Fox, Donkey or Sheep: Political Skills for Managers. *Management Education and Development*, 18(1): 3–19.

Hutchinson, P (2019) Politics in the Workplace: Dealing with Sheep, Donkeys, Foxes and Owls. [online] Available at: https://thinkingfocus.com/politics-in-the-workplace-dealing-with-sheep-donkeys-foxes-and-owls/ (accessed 27 February 2024).

Kennedy, G (2008) *Everything is Negotiable: How to Get the Best Deal Every Time*. New York: Random House.

National Careers Service (nd) Zookeeper. [online] Available at: https://nationalcareers.service.gov.uk/job-profiles/zookeeper (accessed 27 February 2024).

Praxis (nd) Herding Cats. [online] Available at: www.praxisframework.org/en/resource-pages/dibartolomeo-herding-cats (accessed 27 February 2024).

Prospects (2023) Zookeeper. [online] Available at: www.prospects.ac.uk/job-profiles/zookeeper (accessed 27 February 2024).

Chapter 28: Y
YOUR PURPOSE AND VALUES

I mentioned in the opening chapter on authenticity that, at the start of the LeadershipPlus module on the Warwick Business School full-time MBA, I share a slide which reads simply:

Who you are is how you lead.

My hope is that over the course of the next 12 months, while the students immerse themselves in study, assignments and job applications, they develop a deep sense of who they are. One of the readings we give the students is a 2010 *Harvard Business Review* article by Clayton Christensen entitled 'How Will You Measure Your Life?' Christensen is best known for coining the term *disruptive innovation* in the 1990s. A disruptive innovation is a technology or process which makes products and services more affordable and accessible, leading to the displacement of established players. For example, the Model T Ford was a car with basic features that was affordable and easy to use. It transformed and expanded the market for automobiles – by the early 1920s, more than half of the cars in the world were Fords.

In 'How Will You Measure Your Life?' Christensen notes three questions that he poses to his own management students at Harvard Business School.

1. How can I be sure that I'll be happy in my career?
2. How can I be sure that my relationships with my spouse and my family become an enduring source of happiness?
3. How can I be sure I'll stay out of jail?

In addressing the first question, Christensen suggests that making money and doing deals isn't as rewarding as building people. He writes:

> *Management is the most noble of professions if it's practiced well. No other occupation offers as many ways to help other learn and grow, take responsibility and be recognized for achievement, and contribute to the success of a team.*
> (Christensen, 2010)

Regarding the second question, Christensen reflects on how he had to think long and hard to clarify his own purpose. This grew out of his religious faith, but he notes that religion isn't the only thing that gives people direction. He says that knowing his purpose in life is *'the single most useful thing I've ever learnt'* (2010). He applied this knowledge every day.

Although his third question above might come across as light-hearted, several of Christensen's contemporaries when he was a student did end up in jail. He discusses one of the key ideas in economics – basing decisions on marginal costs and revenues. However, this can be a very poor guide in making moral choices. The temptation to do something *just this once* may well lead to regret. It's better to stick to your principles 100 per cent of the time rather than 98 per cent of the time. He concludes: *'You've got to define for yourself what you stand for and draw the line in a safe place'* (2010).

Christensen goes on to discuss the importance of humility, and how people who are humble have a high level of self-esteem. (I discuss humility in Chapter 45.) He writes:

> *Generally, you can only be humble if you feel really good about yourself – and you want to help those around you feel really good about themselves, too. When we see people acting in an abusive, arrogant, or demeaning manner*

towards others, their behavior almost always is a symptom of their lack of self-esteem.

(Christensen, 2010)

He ends the article with this final recommendation:

Think about the metric by which your life will be judged, and make a resolution to live every day so that in the end, your life will be judged a success.

(Christensen, 2010)

Your values

We give the full-time MBA students the Christensen article to read in preparation for a workshop on emotional intelligence. As I noted in Chapter 5, the starting point for emotional intelligence is self-awareness. Being clear about the purpose of your life, as Christensen says, is an invaluable guide.

However, not everyone – including many of our students – has this level of clarity on their purpose. During the workshop, we do an exercise to help the students to reflect upon and clarify their values. This is a more accessible topic, which might be a precursor to identifying purpose. As your read the description of the exercise, you might like to do it yourself.

The first step is a piece of silent coaching – silent because we ask the students to write down their answers to some questions rather than saying them aloud. We invite them to note down five answers to each of these questions.

- What is important to you?
- What fulfils you?
- What things upset you, cause you frustration or make you angry?
- What aspects of your life would you find it really hard to live without?

The second step is to read through your answers and identify the values that underpin them. For example, you might have written that helping others is both important to you and also fulfils you. *Helping others* might, therefore, be one of your key values. Or, to give another example, you might have written that you get upset or angry when you witness people being treated unfairly. Hence, *fairness* might be another of your important values.

We ask each student to identify the eight values that are most important to them, and then to rank these in order of importance.

The third step is to invite the students in pairs to talk through their eight most important values, considering two further questions.

1. On a scale of 1 (not at all) to 10 (very well), how well is each of your values currently being honoured in your life?
2. Choose two values that you would like to honour more effectively. What might you do to realise each of these two values more fully in your life?

Values are often fairly stable – although, as you move through life, your values may shift. For example, career success could be most important to you when you begin work, but work–life balance might become more important once you have a family. Or, someone who has recovered from a serious accident or illness might decide that health and well-being is their number one priority.

> **VIDEOS**
>
> How Will You Measure Your Life? Clay Christensen at TEDxBoston (TEDx Talks, 2012): www.youtube.com/watch?v=tvos4nORf_Y

In this 20-minute TED talk, Clayton Christensen discussed disruptive innovation before going on to consider how to measure your life. The whole video is interesting and engaging, but, if you only want to view the latter topic, join the video after 16 minutes and 56 seconds.

How to Know Your Life Purpose in 5 Minutes – Adam Leipzig at TEDxMalibu (TEDx Talks, 2013): www.youtube.com/watch?v=vVsXO9brK7M

In this ten-minute TED talk, Adam Leipzig takes you through five questions to help you to discover your life purpose. He notes that three of the questions are about other people.

1. Who are you?
2. What do you do?
3. Who do you do it for?
4. What do those people want and need?
5. How do they change as a result?

Reference

Christensen, C (2010) How Will You Measure Your Life? *Harvard Business Review*, July–August. [online] Available at: https://hbr.org/2010/07/how-will-you-measure-your-life (accessed 27 February 2024).

Chapter 29: X

GENERATION X AND GENERATION Y

I am part of the Baby Boomer generation that was born in the years between the end of the Second World War and the mid-1960s. The name reflects the fact that there was a boom in the number of children born into that post-war world. This generation grew up in a period of relative economic stability and prosperity, on the one hand, and a lot of social change, on the other. People of this generation are characterised as optimistic, independent, disciplined and competitive. They have a strong sense of community, a strong work ethic and like structure. They want to climb the ladder of success, seeking status and financial rewards.

Clearly, this description is a generalisation – not everyone born in that era has these characteristics. The assumption that people born within a certain period share similar views and preferences might be more useful in marketing than in psychology. However, generational theory can be a useful way of thinking about society, rather than the absolute truth. As you read this chapter, you may wish to consider how accurate the typologies and the descriptions seem to you.

The idea of generations leads to the notion of a generation gap – differences in attitudes and values between older and younger people. This could be in general within a society, or it might be within an individual family.

Generation X

Generation X is the name given to people born between the mid-1960s and around 1980. Many grew up in a family where both parents were working, and hence they experienced more independence and freedom than previous generations. Independence, self-reliance and resilience are key characteristics of this generation. Social trends such as immigration and a growing female workforce meant they were more diverse.

Generation X faced a more difficult economic landscape than the Baby Boomers, and many found obtaining and retaining a job harder. They were more likely to be laid off, restructured or outsourced. Hence, they were adaptable and willing to accept change in the workplace. They were prepared to change jobs to get ahead, but less likely to job-hop than the succeeding generation. They were keen to work hard, quietly getting on with the job and delivering results without making a fuss – they're sometimes called the silent generation. Although some were workaholics, the generation valued work–life balance more than the Baby Boomer generation.

Generation X grew up in an analogue world and worked in a digital world. They have been described as *'Tech-savvy ... but not Tech-dependent'* (DCI, 2023). They understand the digital world and the impact of technological innovation, and are technically flexible, but they aren't as preoccupied with technology as the succeeding generation are.

Generation Y

Generation Y were born between the early 1980s and the mid-1990s. They are also known as Millennials because the generation began to become adults around the time of the millennium. They are digital natives – they grew up in the internet age, and use mobile devices, digital technology and social media extensively for shopping, entertainment and keeping up with friends.

Although they grew up in a period of stability and economic prosperity, events such as the 11 September attacks in 2001, wars in the Middle East and the deep economic crisis after 2008 changed things. Recession, technological change and global competition meant that many faced unemployment or had to take jobs that did not match their qualifications. They are the first modern generation to be economically worse off than their parents. Partly because of this – but also because of changes in society – millennials are getting married and having children later in life.

Generation Y are regarded as tolerant of others, and open-minded on issues such as race, gender and sexuality. They have a strong sense of social responsibility and concern for the environment. They often seek to have a positive impact on the world. They can be confident, independent, adaptable and ambitious. They may question authority, often seek out new challenges, and want meaningful work. They value work–life balance, and wish to enjoy life outside of work. They may seek to work for organisations whose values align with their personal beliefs.

However, Generation Y are sometimes seen as being narcissistic and spoilt, with a strong need for instant gratification and a sense of entitlement. In 2014, *Time* magazine labelled them the '*me-me-me generation*'.

A note on Generation Z

Generation Z are the people who were born after the mid-1990s. They came of age at a time of pandemic and lockdown, in a world facing huge environmental challenges such as global warming and the loss of biodiversity. They are again a generation of digital natives who spend much of their time online.

Generation Z have the highest prevalence of mental illness of any generation. A McKinsey survey found that:

A series of consumer surveys and interviews conducted by McKinsey indicate stark differences among generations, with Gen Z reporting the least positive life outlook, including lower levels of emotional and social well-being than older generations. One in four Gen Z respondents reported feeling more emotionally distressed (25 percent), almost double the levels reported by millennial and Gen X respondents (13 percent each), and more than triple the levels reported by baby boomer respondents (8 percent). And the COVID-19 pandemic has only amplified this challenge.

(McKinsey, 2022)

In my own role as a senior tutor for half of the final year undergraduates at Warwick Business School (most of whom belong to Generation Z), I have been struck by how many (although far from all) of our students suffer from poor mental health and report that they feel stressed, anxious or depressed. My impression is that the pressure to get a good degree and job, and the pervasive influence of social media, are two of the factors that underlie this. Many of our students are from overseas, and the lack of family and friends close by is also a contributing factor.

VIDEO

Leadership: Gen X and Gen Y (Jennifer Wilson, 2016): www.ifac.org/knowledge-gateway/developing-accountancy-profession/discussion/leadership-gen-x-and-gen-y

In this four-minute video Jennifer Wilson offers some guidance to Generation X leaders and considers how to maximise the contributions of Generation Y.

References

DCI (2023) How to Tailor Retail Experience for Gen X, Millenials & Gen Z. LinkedIn. [online] Available at: www.linkedin.com/pulse/how-tailor-retail-experience-gen-x-millennials-z-dci-marketing-cayfc (accessed 5 March 2024).

McKinsey (2022) Addressing the Unprecedented Behavioral-health Challenges Facing Generation Z. [online] Available at: www.mckinsey.com/industries/healthcare/our-insights/addressing-the-unprecedented-behavioral-health-challenges-facing-generation-z (accessed 27 February 2024).

Chapter 30: W

WELL-BEING IN THE WORKPLACE

There are a number of aspects of well-being in the workplace, including safety and physical health, social well-being, financial and career well-being and mental well-being. These are interlinked – for instance, physical health can impact on mental health. In this chapter I shall focus on mental health and well-being in the workplace, looking at what individuals can do to manage their mental well-being, and what a manager can do to support them in this.

Introducing the Health and Safety Executive's annual statistics on work-related ill-health and injury for 2021/22 (UKATA, 2022), chief executive Sarah Albon said:

> *Stress and poor mental health is the number one cause of work-related ill health. The effects of stress, depression, and anxiety can have a significant impact on an employee's life and on their ability to perform their best at work.*

The estimated number of workers in Great Britain suffering a work-related illness that year was 1.8 million, with stress, depression and anxiety making up around half of the cases (Health and Safety Executive, 2023).

Individual mental well-being

I mentioned at the end of the previous chapter that I frequently meet with students who are struggling with mental health issues. I am very clear about the boundaries of my role here – I am not a professional well-being adviser or counsellor. Hence, I often encourage students to contact the university's well-being team which offer a variety of resources, including self-help materials, classes and individual counselling or therapy.

I would similarly encourage any employee struggling with mental health problems to seek professional support. Speaking to your GP is often the first step. They might prescribe appropriate medication, and may also make a referral for some form of talking therapy. Nearly 1.2 million people accessed support from NHS Talking Therapies in England in 2021/22 (NHS, nd).

Unfortunately, the waiting time to see a counsellor or therapist can be long. It's also possible to arrange to see a counsellor or therapist privately – although many people may not be able to afford this. A useful first step is to look up the list of counsellors and therapists who have been accredited by the British Association for Counselling and Psychotherapy on the BACP website (see www.bacp.co.uk/search/Therapists). It is easy to filter the list of counsellors by location if someone wishes to have sessions in person rather than online.

Having written these paragraphs, I am aware of the paradox that someone who really needs to share their struggles with a professional may be extremely reluctant to do so. The website of the mental health charity Mind describes the following five areas where someone can take some simple steps to improve their mental well-being, feel more positive and get more out of life.

Step 1 – Connect

Connecting with others can help us feel close to people, and valued for who we are. Being social means different things for different people – you might prefer being in quieter situations with one other person, or you might like being in big groups. You might like to connect with people online, or you might enjoy phone calls or sending letters.

Step 2 – Get active

Many people find that physical activity helps them maintain positive mental health. This doesn't have to mean running marathons or training every day at the gym. There are lots of different things you can do to be a bit more active. Studies have shown that getting active can help you sleep better, have happier moods, and reduce feelings of stress, anxiety and racing thoughts.

Step 3 – Take notice

Reminding yourself to take notice can help you to be aware of how you're feeling. It can help you understand what triggers your feelings of stress or anxiety. Some studies have shown that savouring 'the moment' can also help you to feel more positive about life. Take some time to enjoy the moment and the environment around you.

Step 4 – Learn

We're always learning new things – often without realising it. Feeling like you're learning and developing can boost your self-esteem. And sometimes, setting goals can help you to feel more productive and more in control of your life.

Step 5 – Give

There's been lots of research about the effects of taking part in social and community life. Some studies have shown that people who help others are more likely to rate themselves as happy.

(Mind, nd)

Support from a manager

Another aspect of my role is that I act as a mediator when two members of staff at the University of Warwick are in some form of conflict with one another. It is frequently the case that the disagreement is between an individual and their line manager. I know that there are always two stories in any mediation. Often, what the manager sees as appropriate performance management is viewed by the individual as bullying or harassment. Thus, it can be the case that, as a manager, you yourself are the cause of stress and anxiety felt by someone who reports to you. In writing that sentence, I am making a general statement, not attempting to judge in any way the legitimacy of a managerial action.

On the other hand, as a manager, you may be in a good position to help someone who is struggling with their mental well-being. Here are some things that you might usefully do.

- Reflect upon your own style of management, and consider how this impacts the different individuals who report to you, some of whom will be more resilient than others.
- Think about the practicalities of the working environment, both on site and regarding arrangements for remote working in today's hybrid environment.
- Continually look out for signs that someone may be struggling. Pay attention to changes in someone's performance or behaviour.
- Reach out to anyone who does seem to be struggling. Show that you're there to listen with empathy and, if possible, without judgement. Check in with them regularly.
- Sometimes listening is all you can do – and this may be enough. However, there may be practical help you can give or arrange. It might be appropriate to encourage the person to reach out for professional support.
- Be willing to share aspects of your own situation. There is still a lot of stigma in society attached to mental illness. You can't remove this, but you might be able to set a tone where it's okay to be vulnerable.
- Reflect too upon the climate within your department. For example, how reasonable are the expectations around working long hours, taking holidays, being present in the office?

- To what extent do individuals look out for one another and to what extent is there an unhealthy spirit of rivalry or competitiveness?
- Support the learning and development, and the realistic career aspirations, of each member of your team.

As a manager, you will be operating within a wider corporate culture. If the culture of your organisation is toxic in some way – for instance, if there is an assumption that people will work very long hours – you will be limited in how far you can create a healthier sub-culture within your team. I shall be discussing organisational culture in Chapter 38.

> **VIDEO**
>
> Dying for a Paycheck (The Busy Reader, 2018): www.youtube.com/watch?v=XaPaNA7W3iY
>
> This three-minute video introduces Jeffrey Pfeffer's book, *Dying for a Paycheck*, which has the subtitle, *How Modern Management Harms Employee Health and Company Performance – and What We Can Do About It*. Pfeffer says that what makes a great place to work isn't the perks, the mission or the prestige. Rather, it's job control and autonomy, and social support.

References

Health and Safety Executive (2023) HSE Publishes Annual Work-related Ill Health and Injury Statistics for 2022/23. [online] Available at: https://press.hse.gov.uk/2023/11/22/hse-publishes-annual-work-related-ill-health-and-injury-statistics-for-2022-23/ (accessed 27 February 2024).

Mind (nd) 5 Ways to Wellbeing. [online] Available at: www.mind.org.uk/workplace/mental-health-at-work/five-ways-to-wellbeing/ (accessed 27 February 2024).

NHS (nd) NHS Talking Therapies, for Anxiety and Depression. [online] Available at: https://www.england.nhs.uk/mental-health/adults/nhs-talking-therapies/ (accessed 3 June 2024).

Pfeffer, J (2018) *Dying for a Paycheck: How Modern Management Harms Employee Health and Company Performance – and What We Can Do About It*. New York: HarperCollins.

UKATA (2022) HSE Publishes Annual Work-Related Ill-Health and Injury Statistics for 2021/22. [online] Available at: www.ukata.org.uk/news/hse-publishes-annual-work-related-ill-health-and-injury-statistics-202122 (accessed 5 March 2024).

Chapter 31: V
VISION AND STRATEGY

When I worked at the British Gas Management Centre, we ran a one-week course for the company's senior managers. The Monday morning was devoted to a session on strategy, delivered by someone from a leading business school. Several decades later, the key thing I remember from that session is that the word *strategy* comes from the Greek word *strategos*, meaning a general. To think and act strategically is akin to taking on the role of a general – being clear about the ultimate goal, creating a plan of action and delegating the carrying out of that plan to others. I think it's a very useful metaphor.

The starting point for creating a strategy is a vision for the future. This articulates what the organisation wants to become and to be recognised for. It is often expressed as an inspirational and engaging statement. Although it may be broad, a good vision statement is succinct.

Here are some examples of vision statements from well-known organisations.

- Google: To provide access to the world's information in one click.
- Nike: To bring inspiration and innovation to every athlete in the world.
- Oxfam: A just and sustainable world.
- IKEA: To create a better everyday life for the many people.

- BBC: To act in the public interest, serving all audiences through the provision of impartial, high-quality and distinctive output and services which inform, educate and entertain.
- Ben & Jerry's: We believe that ice cream can change the world.

On their website, Ben & Jerry's go on to set out how they want their vision to support the needs of a range of stakeholders.

We believe that ice cream can change the world. We have a progressive, nonpartisan social mission that seeks to meet human needs and eliminate injustices in our local, national, and international communities by integrating these concerns in our day-to-day business activities.

(Ben & Jerry's, nd)

Similarly, Oxfam expand the statement of their vision to paint an ambitious picture of the future they wish to create:

We have a vision of a just and sustainable world. A world where people and the planet are at the center of our economy. Where women and girls live free from violence and discrimination. Where the climate crisis is contained. And where governance systems are inclusive and allow for those in power to be held to account.

(Oxfam International, 2024)

Statements such as these come from the leaders of an organisation. The vision should, in turn, act as a guide for managers and employees throughout the business. While it is likely to be aspirational and challenging, a vision needs to be feasible and practical. It also has to be communicated well, both to employees and to other stakeholders.

If you are a middle manager within an organisation, you do not have the scope to set such ambitious aspirations, and you need to work within parameters set by the leaders of the business. Nevertheless, you might still have a vision for how you wish your team to operate and what you want it to achieve. And, just as the vision of an organisation should engage and perhaps inspire its members, so too your vision for your department can help to motivate and focus the efforts of your people.

Strategy

As I noted earlier, a clear statement of the vision is the starting point for creating a strategy for the organisation. A strategy sets out the direction and scope of the organisation, and how it will deploy resources to meet the needs of customers and other stakeholders.

In a large organisation, strategy will be created at different levels. There will be an overall corporate strategy, which will include a structure of, for example, business units operating in different industries or territories. Each business unit is likely to have its own strategy, which will express how it deploys resources and people. Corporate strategy provides the framework within which business strategies operate. Individual teams or departments within each business unit may have a strategy on how they will contribute successfully to the overall corporate and business unit strategy. Strategy at the different levels should be aligned to promote the success of the organisation. This might be achieved by cascading objectives down the organisation.

A great advantage in having a clear strategy is that it makes decisions for you. It guides you on which activities are really important, which are less so and which don't need to happen at all. This helps you to decide where to focus your time and effort. It applies to individuals too. For example, if you know where you want to be in your career in five years' time, say, this helps you choose which jobs to apply for or what learning opportunities to pursue. It also guides you on things that you don't need to spend much (or any) time on.

In an article entitled 'How to Turn a Strategic Vision into Reality', Kara Baskin (2018) notes how companies often get lost in jargon or in creating overly detailed long-term plans. She offers these pointers on how to balance, on the one hand, providing enough guidance to staff and, on the other, allowing flexibility to enable people to adapt or seize opportunities.

- **Limit your objectives to a handful.** *This forces you to focus on what matters most and make important trade-offs among conflicting objectives.*

- **Focus on the midterm.** *Priorities usually take three to five years to accomplish. Annual goals are too tactical, and long-term goals are too abstract to offer real guidance.*

- **Pull toward the future.** *Rather than concentrating on what worked well in the past.*

- **Make the hard calls.** *Strategy is about choice.*

- **Address critical vulnerabilities.** *Pay attention to the key priorities that might fail in execution.*

- **Provide concrete guidance.** *On where to focus and on what to stop doing.*

- **Align the top team.** *Surprisingly often, managers can't name their company's strategic priorities.*

(Baskin, 2018)

> **RESOURCE**
>
> Ten Things We Know to Be True (Google, nd): https://about.google/philosophy/
>
> Many organisations translate their vision into a statement of corporate values. In my own experience of working in a number of organisations, statements of values are often

more about rhetoric than reality. I also resent the idea that someone will tell me what my values should be. For example, I'm happy to be told that customer focus is important and that my organisation expects me to focus on the needs of our customers. While I'm willing to behave in a customer-focused way, don't tell me that it's a value of mine.

I've never worked in Google, so I can't comment on what the employees of the company believe about its values. However, since its early days Google has been known for its belief in these ten things.

1. Focus on the user and all else will follow.
2. It's best to do one thing really, really well.
3. Fast is better than slow.
4. Democracy on the web works.
5. You don't need to be at your desk to need an answer.
6. You can make money without doing evil.
7. There's always more information out there.
8. The need for information crosses all borders.
9. You can be serious without a suit.
10. Great just isn't good enough.

References

Baskin, K (2018) How to Turn a Strategic Vision into Reality. MIT Management School. [online] Available at: https://mitsloan.mit.edu/ideas-made-to-matter/how-to-turn-a-strategic-vision-reality (accessed 27 February 2024).

Ben & Jerry's (nd) Our Values, Activism and Mission. [online] Available at: www.benjerry.co.uk/values (accessed 27 February 2024).

Oxfam International (2024) What We Believe. [online] Available at: www.oxfam.org/en/what-we-do/about/what-we-believe#:~:text=We%20have%20a%20vision%20of,free%20from%20violence%20and%20discrimination (accessed 27 February 2024).

Chapter 32: U
UNDERSTANDING CONTEXT

In the previous chapter I noted how having a clear vision of where an organisation wishes to go is a vital step in creating a strategy. It's also important to have a well-informed understanding of where the organisation currently is and to consider how the environment might change over the coming years. This is also true if you're looking to create a strategy and action plan for your team or department, rather than for an entire organisation. As I noted in Chapter 27, appreciating the internal politics of your organisation is often an important part of the context.

In Chapter 28 I mentioned briefly Clayton Christensen's idea of disruptive innovation, which is a technology or process that leads to the displacement of established players. A look along any high street in Britian today shows how many businesses have closed or moved because of competition from online shopping and the impact of lockdowns. A successful strategy needs to anticipate the trends that will shape the future environment. It also needs to take into account factors such as the impact of Brexit, and be able to respond to unanticipated events such as the war in Ukraine.

We live today in a VUCA world – that is a business environment that is volatile, uncertain, complex and ambiguous.

- **Volatile** – many things are changing, often quickly and unpredictably. For example, over the past few years energy prices, raw material costs and interest rates have been extremely volatile.

- **Uncertain** – the present is unclear, while the future is uncertain and hard to predict. It may be difficult to understand cause and effect, and the past may be a poor guide to the future.
- **Complex** – our world is more complex than ever, and it is becoming harder to understand problems and the impact of change. There is a high level of interconnection of everything around us.
- **Ambiguous** – there is a lack of clarity or awareness about situations, and the demands on businesses may be contradictory or paradoxical. This makes decision-making more difficult, and may necessitate the willingness to risk making mistakes.

Creating a strategy – and translating this into practical action steps – is thus much more challenging today than when times were more stable. Let's look at two frameworks – PESTLE and SWOT – which have been used for many years in strategic analysis and are still useful tools in today's VUCA environment.

PESTLE

The PESTLE framework offers a structure for identifying the key factors in the business environment that will have an impact on the fortunes of the organisation. It is used especially in marketing to assess threats and opportunities which need to be taken into account in setting and implementing a strategy.

The acronym stands for political, economic, social, technological, legal, environmental.

Political

Political factors include the impact of government policies and regulation, and relevant laws which need to be complied with. For example, changes in taxation, import restrictions, new trading arrangements and political instability might be important influences on business activities.

Economic

The outlook for the economy – for example, growth rates, prospects for consumer spending, exchange rates, inflation and interest rates – are very likely to impact on the activities and profitability of a business.

Social

Social factors such as demographic trends or changes in consumer attitudes and lifestyles may heavily influence the sales of an organisation. For example, as people become more conscious of eating more healthily, this will boost sales of some products and hit sales of others.

Technological

All organisations use technology, some more than others. As well as developments in specific technologies, general trends in innovation and automation will impact organisations. For example, the growth of internet shopping has created massive changes in the retail industry. And artificial intelligence is going to have an enormous impact on many organisations.

Legal

Legal factors may overlap with political factors. They include things like employment laws, health and safety regulations, data privacy and consumer protection. A specific illustration might be the importance of patents to protect a company's intellectual property.

Environmental

One of the key features in today's VUCA world is the widening realisation of the importance of environmental factors such as climate change and sustainability. Organisations need to pay careful attention to the whole lifecycle of their products – supply chains, production, selling and waste disposal.

SWOT

The SWOT framework, which can be used alongside a PESTLE analysis, is a tool for assessing the strengths and weaknesses of an organisation and the opportunities and threats in its business environment. I like to think of strengths and weaknesses as primarily internal to the organisation, while opportunities and threats are external. A SWOT analysis can help to align the goals and activities of the organisation with the evolving external context. It can also be used as a guide in managing a project or in decision-making – perhaps in identifying blindspots or in recognising strengths that could be capitalised on more fully.

- **Strengths:** these are the things that the organisation does well and the distinctive resources that it can draw upon.
- **Weaknesses:** these are the things that the organisation does less well or where it has fewer resources than competitors. They may be areas where the organisation can improve.
- **Opportunities:** these are the possibilities and trends in the external environment which the organisation could capitalise upon.
- **Threats:** these are external factors which pose risks to the organisation and its strategy. They may be things that the competition is doing. It may be necessary to create contingency plans in case the threats do materialise.

To carry out a SWOT analysis, a good starting point is to gather together a suitable group of stakeholders who are aware of different aspects of the situation. It can then be useful to brainstorm ideas and thoughts. There is a risk here that the discussion may lose focus and become bogged down in detail. There is also a risk in simply producing a long list of points. Hence, it is essential to allow time to analyse and assess critically the ideas that have been generated. A meaningful SWOT analysis takes time.

In generating ideas, a further risk is that these may be based on assumptions that turn out to be unfounded, or which are overtaken by the pace of change externally.

> **RESOURCE AND VIDEO**
>
> PESTLE Analysis Examples (On Strategy, 2022): https://onstrategyhq.com/resources/pestle-analysis-examples/
>
> In this article and a five-minute video, Erica Olsen sets out how to conduct a PESTLE analysis. The text includes six PESTLE analyses for Starbucks, Beyond Meat, Walmart, Amazon, Apple and Airbnb.

Chapter 33: T
TALENT MANAGEMENT

When I worked in the gas pipeline company Transco, one of my roles was to set up and facilitate meetings of the senior management team to review and develop the talented people within the business. We had a clear process on how to do this, which is the basis of this chapter. The reality was less impressive, as the management team meetings which were at the heart of the process were often postponed or cancelled. I suspect that a less formal way of identifying and nurturing talent was in play at the same time.

The aim in talent management is to identify the people in the organisation who have more talent than others and then to develop these people so that they become more experienced and competent, able to play a greater part in the success of the organisation.

The key questions that need to be addressed are as follows.

- What are the attributes that we are looking for to identify who is talented?
- Which of our employees have – or could develop – these attributes?
- For each of these talented individuals, what actions are needed to nurture their development?

To answer the first question, it's important that the management team can articulate what they mean by talent – what are the qualities or behaviours that make someone more talented than their contemporaries? Otherwise, there is a risk that *talented* may implicitly equate to *someone like us*. It's helpful too to share this articulation with the employees of the organisation so that people know what is being sought.

Many companies use a competency framework as the basis for this. Here is an example.

Table 33.1 Competency framework example

Vision	Articulating future possibilities that will transform the current situation.
Drive	Having the will, ambition, energy and resilience to stand out from the crowd and proactively make things happen.
Personal presence	Demonstrating the self-confidence, gravitas and ability to speak convincingly that influences people and events.
Integrity	Acting consistently with a clear set of personal values that includes dealing with others fairly and honestly.
Judgement	Using a blend of common sense, intuition, wisdom and analytical skills to make high quality decisions.
Emotional intelligence	Having a high awareness of the feelings of self and others, together with the self-control and social skills to interact effectively with most people.

There are two key steps which are very helpful in answering the second question. The first is to have a meaningful process for individuals to have an honest development review conversation with their line manager. The word *meaningful* is key here – in many organisations the annual review process is regarded as a ritual that requires the completion of paperwork to be returned to the HR department. Assuming that these conversations are meaningful, then assessments of capability can be shared further up the organisation. The second step is for the management team to have a talent review meeting which considers the feedback from individual reviews in order to form a shared picture of who are the individuals that they wish to nurture and promote. (Note that it's important to develop other people too, not just those identified as talented.) The list of those regarded as talented is often treated as confidential – one advantage is that it doesn't send a signal to everyone else that they're not talented.

There are a number of things that can be done to address the third question. In Chapter 7 I discussed how deep and sustained learning requires experience, coupled with reflection to learn from experience. I noted the words of Morgan McCall (1998): *'The principle is simple: people learn most by doing things they haven't done before.'*

The most valuable development experiences in the workplace usually come from tackling a new job. Thus, a talent review meeting provides an opportunity to discuss who to move into new roles within the organisation. McCall writes:

> *Because such a large number of the experiences important to the development of executive leadership skills occur through work assignments, the critical question is clearly, 'Who gets what job?'*
>
> (McCall, 1998)

While a new and challenging job provides the richest vehicle for development, there are other ways of giving people opportunities to build their capability. A secondment to a new role or the chance to lead a major project will provide real-time experiences for development.

Having set up an opportunity for a talented individual to take part in a challenging experience, it is also important to ensure that they have the chance to reflect on and make sense of the experience. Having constructive feedback conversations on their performance and progress is vital.

Another intervention often used to nurture talent is to offer the individual the chance to work with a coach or a mentor. This might be in parallel with a new job opportunity, or it might be simply for someone who is progressing within the organisation without necessarily being part of a talent management process.

A further possibility is to invite the individual to take part in a leadership development programme. This might be an internal programme within the organisation, or it could be an external programme such as those offered by many business schools.

A vital foundation for a successful talent management process in an organisation is the commitment of the person at the top. Unless they are genuinely committed to making talent management effective, then it won't really work. An illustration of a chief executive who took leadership development seriously is Larry Bossidy. As CEO of the US firm AlliedSignal, Bossidy transformed the fortunes of the company. He reckons that he spent between 30 per cent and 40 per cent of his time in the first two years hiring and developing leaders. He writes in the *Harvard Business Review* that:

> *I'm convinced that AlliedSignal's success was due in large part to the amount of time and emotional commitment I devoted to leadership development.*
>
> *Many executives have neglected a personal involvement, accountability, and initiative in developing leaders within their organizations. But because it is full of unknowns, of unpredictability, it deserves more time than anything else you do as CEO.*
>
> (Bossidy, 2001)

> **RESOURCE**
>
> Talent Management (CIPD, 2023): www.cipd.org/uk/knowledge/factsheets/talent-factsheet/
>
> This factsheet from the Chartered Institute of Personnel and Development sets out a wider view of a talent management strategy.

References

Bossidy, L (2001) The Job No CEO Should Delegate. *Harvard Business Review* March. [online] Available at: https://hbr.org/2001/03/the-job-no-ceo-should-delegate#:~:text=It%27s%20impossible%20to%20spend%20too,cultivating%20his%20firm%27s%20future%20leaders (accessed 27 February 2024).

McCall, M (1998) *High Flyers: Developing the Next Generation of Leaders*. Boston: Harvard Business School.

Chapter 34: S

SHADOW OF THE LEADER

I first came across the term *shadow of the leader* in the mid-1990s when I attended a culture change programme that was being rolled out throughout Transco. Transco had just been split off as a result of the demerger of British Gas. As the owner of the gas pipeline network throughout Great Britain, Transco remained a natural monopoly. Our first managing director, Harry Moulson, was keen to establish a customer-focused and empowered culture. He brought in the Senn Delaney organisation to lead a very successful culture change programme. (I'll discuss organisational culture in Chapter 38.)

In a post entitled 'What Leadership Shadow Do You Cast?' Jim Hart and Larry Senn (from the Senn Delaney organisation) write:

> The shadow phenomenon exists for anyone who is a leader of any group, including a parent in a family. That is because people tend to take on the characteristics of those who have power or influence over them.
>
> The role of the leader, at work and at home, requires modeling the desired behavior and letting others see the desired values in action. To become effective leaders, we must become aware of our shadows and then learn to have our actions match our message.
>
> (Hart and Senn, 2016)

The term *leadership shadow* was coined by the investment bank Goldman Sachs. It refers to the inevitable impact that the actions and words of a manager has on the people who report to them.

The messages you send – and how people perceive them – create a shadow. As a leader, you cannot not cast a shadow. And people take meaning both from what you do and also what you don't do as a leader.

There are four elements that contribute to your leadership shadow.

1. **What you say** – both your written and your spoken words, and also perhaps the non-verbal cues that you send.
2. **How you act** – your behaviours, positive and negative, which may serve to act as a role model for others.
3. **What you prioritise** – how you actually spend your time sends important signals.
4. **What you measure** – the key things that you hold people accountable for, and how you recognise and reward them.

It's important to understand the shadow that you produce and the impact it has on others. It may be difficult to see clearly the shape and reach of the shadow that you cast. You may wish to take a step back and ask yourself if you consciously manage the messages you are sending. And you might seek feedback from others – perhaps by undertaking a 360-degree feedback exercise – on how they perceive you and the impact on them and the business of the shadow that you create.

The further up you are in the hierarchy of your organisation, the wider the shadow that you cast. Leadership starts at the top, and if leaders want to make a difference, they in particular must understand the shadow they produce. Their actions, decisions and communications crucially affect the culture of the entire enterprise. Jim Hart and Larry Senn end the post mentioned earlier with these two paragraphs:

> *As a firm that specializes in culture shaping, Senn Delaney has an unwritten policy that we won't design or conduct a*

> culture-shaping architecture for clients unless we can first work with the team that leads the organization, or a major semi-autonomous group, and its leader. It's not that we don't want the business; it's just that we know that without a positive leadership shadow, the process is unlikely to work.
>
> In order to build a winning culture, the top teams must be seen by the organization as living the values and walking the talk. Based on the size of the organization, it is usually the top 100 to 500 people that really set the culture.
>
> (Hart and Senn, 2016)

I mentioned in the opening paragraph that the culture change programme in Transco was successful. Everyone in the organisation, including the managing director, Harry Moulson, and his management team attended a three-day culture change workshop. Each manager attended two of these – one with their peers and their own boss, and another with the team that they led. To give an illustration of how they 'walked the talk', none of the directors had a private office – they all worked in an open-plan office in our headquarters in Solihull. Any member of staff who wished to could enter their wing of the building to speak with any of the directors. This openness was part of the shadow that Harry and his colleagues sought to create. Since there were times when Harry needed to concentrate on important matters, he had a rule that if he was at his desk and wearing his baseball hat, this meant that he was busy and couldn't be disturbed.

Shadow of the manager

The discussion above has focused on the shadow cast by those at the top of an organisation, and its impact on the culture of the enterprise. However, someone who is managing, say, a small department still produces a shadow that their people will work under. If you are such a manager, it's worth your while thinking consciously about the shadow that you cast and seeking feedback on the impact that you have. And considering what you might say or do differently to adjust your shadow.

There is one other aspect that I'd like to mention. As a manager, you are likely to be seen as some form of authority figure. I think that some people project all sorts of things onto their boss. I suspect that often this reflects – probably unconsciously – their feelings towards their own parents and their childhood experiences with authority figures. I touched on this in Chapter 2 and the idea from Transactional Analysis of Parent, Adult and Child ego states. I think that the expectations which people have of their manager are often unrealistic. This isn't fair, but I believe it's the reality. I sometimes sum this up in a phrase – please excuse my wording here – that as a manager, *ex officio*, you inevitably pick up a pile of shit!

> **VIDEO**
>
> Your Leadership Shadow (The Values Partnership, 2023): www.youtube.com/watch?v=0rlTcB9Iz3M
>
> In this four-minute video Miles Protter discusses the importance of being aware of the shadow that you cast as a leader through the impact of what you say, do and reinforce (and don't say, do or reinforce).

Reference

Hart, J and Senn, L (2016) What Leadership Shadow Do You Cast? SmartBrief. [online] Available at: www.smartbrief.com/original/what-leadership-shadow-do-you-cast#:~:text=To%20become%20effective%20leaders%2C%20we,our%20actions%20match%20our%20message.&text=The%20head%20of%20an%20organization,powerful%2C%20yet%20it%20always%20exists (accessed 27 February 2024).

Chapter 35: R

ROMANCE OF LEADERSHIP AND FOLLOWERSHIP

The term *romance of leadership* was coined by James Meindl and colleagues in an article in 1985. The term reflects the tendency – among leadership scholars, practitioners, the media and society – to see leadership as the most important factor shaping the success or failure of organisations. The role of the leader is overemphasised in explaining the performance of an enterprise, while other factors – such as the contribution of followers or changes in the external business environment – are neglected. Meindl et al (1985) write:

> *It appears that as observers of and as participants in organizations, we may have developed highly romanticized, heroic views of leadership – what leaders do, what they are able to accomplish, and the general effects they have on our lives.*

A good illustration of the romance of leadership is the case of Fred Goodwin. He was the CEO of the Royal Bank of Scotland (RBS) group from 2001 to 2009. He presided over an aggressive expansion of the group through a series of acquisitions. He was named 'Businessman of the Year' by *Forbes* magazine, and received a knighthood for his services to banking. However, the takeover of the Dutch bank ABM Amro in the autumn of 2007 coincided with the start of the global financial crisis and was a disaster which led to the near-collapse of the group – the government had to step in to save the bank by, in effect, nationalising it. Goodwin was forced to resign, and his knighthood was annulled in 2012.

The rise and fall of Goodwin illustrates how he was seen initially as a hero who masterminded the success of RBS and later as the villain who was responsible for its collapse. Both views are an oversimplification of a complex reality. It also illustrates how the press and other media construct a narrative that uncritically puts a leader on a pedestal, as it were – and sometimes knocks them off.

Followership

The romantic view of leadership neglects the contribution of followers, often portraying them as reactive and compliant. Even the terms *leader* and *follower* suggest a notion of inferiority, and might produce a Parent–Child pattern of transactions that become entrenched in the culture of an organisation.

Followership is the ability to support a leader in the achievement of the organisation's goals. It is an active, not a passive, role. In the introduction to her book, *The Courageous Follower*, Ira Chaleff (2009) writes:

> *This book proposes a proactive view of the follower's role, which brings it into parity with the leader's role. Parity is approached when we recognize that leaders rarely use their power wisely or effectively over long periods unless they are supported by followers who have the stature to help them do so.*

As the title of her book states, Chaleff views followership as a conscious act of courage. She sets out a model, summarised in Figure 35.1, based on two different behaviours – the courage to support the leader and the courage to challenge the leader. This produces four styles of followership.

1. **Resource:** someone who will not challenge or support the leader, possibly someone who does the minimum needed to keep their job.

2. **Individualist:** someone who offers little support but is happy to challenge the leader's policies or behaviour – may well be argumentative or aggressive, and likely to be marginalised.
3. **Implementer:** someone who is happy to support the leader but isn't willing to challenge, even when the leader is mistaken – sees their role as to follow orders without questioning.
4. **Partner:** someone who will support and challenge a leader because they believe that they have a stake in the leader's decisions – willing to dissent clearly when appropriate – ultimately able to provide the best support to the leader.

Figure 35.1 A model of followership

	High support	
Low challenge	Implementer | Partner	High challenge
	Resource | Individualist	
	Low support	

Source: Chaleff, 2009

Chaleff explores a number of dimensions of courage which followers can exhibit – the courage to assume responsibility, the courage to serve, the courage to challenge, the courage to participate in transformation and the courage to take moral action. In regard to the final point, she writes:

> *Courageous followers know when it is time to take a stand that is different than that of the leader's. They are answering to a higher set of values. The stand may involve refusing*

to obey a direct order, appealing the order to the next level of authority, or tendering one's resignation.
(Chaleff, 2009)

Psychoanalytic theories of leadership

I noted at the end of the previous chapter my own view that people often view their manager as some form of authority figure in a way that reflects unconsciously their own early childhood experiences. Some writers on leadership draw on psychoanalytic theory to develop their ideas. They suggest that someone's style of leadership will be influenced by the models of leadership they experienced in childhood, through adolescence and into adulthood. Moreover, the way in which we are raised may well influence the way in which we choose to follow, including how we react to, on the one hand, an authoritarian manager and, on the other, a participative manager.

Psychoanalytic explanations may also help to understand how people tolerate working for a leader who is toxic. An extreme example of this might be a following a cult leader or a religious fundamentalist. I wonder how far it might account for the electoral success of a number of populist politicians who have led governments in a number of countries over recent years.

RESOURCE

Beware the Romance of Leadership (Leonard Wong and Stephen Gerras, 2017): https://warontherocks.com/2017/02/beware-the-romance-of-leadership/

In this article, Leonard Wong and Stephen Gerras discuss several examples from the US military and political scene. They note that romanticising the role of the leader makes →

> it easier to make sense of the world but can also mislead us into overlooking the true causes of success or failure. They add that leaders who are perceived as charismatic are more likely to be romanticised. They also observe that leadership is romanticised more where power and prestige are concentrated at the top of an organisation.

References

Chaleff, I (2009) *The Courageous Follower: Standing Up to and For Our Leaders*. San Francisco: Berrett-Koehler.

Meindl, J, Ehrlich, S and Dukerich, M (1985) The Romance of Leadership. *Administrative Science Quarterly*, 30(1): 78–102.

Chapter 36: Q
QUIET LEADERSHIP

In the previous chapter on the romance of leadership, I noted how many leadership scholars and the media place an undue emphasis on the importance of a leader in shaping the success or failure of organisations. It is to be expected that a media article on leadership will be based on individuals whom the public have some awareness of – for instance, political leaders such as Margaret Thatcher, Donald Trump or Vladimir Putin, or well-known business leaders such as Richard Branson, Elon Musk or Bill Gates. I imagine that someone who worked closely with any of these individuals would paint a different and more nuanced picture of the impact of their leadership on their immediate followers.

In his book *Leading Quietly: An Unorthodox Guide to Doing the Right Thing*, Joseph Badaracco (2002) contrasts such leaders with what he terms '*quiet leaders*'. Based on his career studying management and leadership, he writes that:

> *the most effective leaders are rarely public heroes. ... They move patiently, carefully, and incrementally. They do what is right – for their organizations, for the people around them, and for themselves – inconspicuously and without casualties.*
>
> (Badaracco, 2002)

He goes on to conclude that:

> *The vast majority of difficult, important human problems – both inside and outside organizations – are not solved by a swift, decisive stroke from someone at the top. What*

usually matters are careful, thoughtful, small, practical efforts by people working far from the limelight. In short, quiet leadership is what moves and changes the world.
(Badaracco, 2002)

You might like to reflect on your own experience of people in organisations that you worked in or with who made things move. To what extent does the heroic view or the quiet view of leadership help to explain how they acted?

In putting together the material for this chapter I came across two very different books with the title *Quiet Leadership*. One is by David Rock (2007), best known for his writing on neuroscience, who coined the term *neuroleadership*. His book explores how a leader can bring out the best in their people by helping them to think rather than telling them what to do. He sets out in considerable detail a six-step framework for transforming performance, based on listening to people, helping them to take a solution-focused approach, speaking succinctly, and encouraging and trusting people to develop their ideas.

The other book with this title is by the highly successful Italian football manager, Carlo Ancelotti. It's really a football book, not a leadership book. But here are two ideas that resonate. He (or maybe his two ghost writers) says, *'players do their best when they are comfortable, not when they are uncomfortable'* (Ancelotti et al, 2017). And also, reflecting on his experiences working for billionaire club owners: *'Stay humble, because no matter how talented you are, there is almost always someone who can fire you'* (2017).

In Chapter 10 I looked at the four dimensions of the Myers–Briggs Type Indicator, the first of which is the Extravert–Introvert dimension. Extraverts are energised by being with other people, while Introverts prefer to focus on their own inner world. In her bestselling book *Quiet,* which has the subtitle *The Power of Introverts in a World That Can't Stop Talking*, Susan Cain explores how Western culture values Extraversion far more than Introversion. She describes how Extraversion became a cultural ideal in the US. In a chapter entitled 'The Myth of Charismatic Leadership', she discusses the Harvard Business School, suggesting that, '*The essence of the HBS education is that leaders have to act confidently and make decisions in the face of incomplete information*'. She adds that, '*The school also tries hard to turn quiet students into talkers*' (Cain, 2012). I know from conversations I've had with someone who taught at Harvard that active participation in classroom discussions is assessed and contributes significantly to an individual's marks – a practice which favours Extraverts and disadvantages Introverts.

Cain contrasts the idea of charismatic leadership with lessons drawn by Jim Collins from his study of best-performing companies. '*We don't need giant personalities to transform companies. We need leaders who build not their own egos but the institutions they run*' (Cain, 2012).

She goes on to discuss the work of Adam Grant who was a consultant to many leading US executives and military leaders. She summarises:

> *Because of their inclination to listen to others and lack of interest in dominating social situations, introverts are more likely to hear and implement suggestions. Having benefited from the talents of their followers, they are then likely to motivate them to be even more proactive. Introverted leaders create a virtuous circle of proactivity, in other words.*
>
> *Extroverts, on the other hand, can be so intent on putting their own stamp on events that they risk losing others' good ideas along the way and allowing workers to lapse into passivity.*
>
> (Cain, 2012)

In discussing Introverts and Extraverts, it's important to emphasise that the terms reflect individual preferences. They don't assess capability. A great advantage in knowing your own preference is that you may recognise when it's valuable to flex your behaviour, drawing consciously on your less-preferred style.

On her website Susan Cain lists these ten points in a manifesto, *The Quiet Way*.

1. There is a word for 'people who are in their heads too much' – thinkers.

2. Solitude is a catalyst for innovation.

3. The next generation of quiet kids can and must be raised to know their own strengths.

4. Sometimes it helps to be a pretend-extrovert. There is always time to be quiet later.

5. But in the long run, staying true to your temperament is the key to finding work you love and work that matters.

6. One genuine relationship is worth a fistful of business cards.

7. It's okay to cross the street to avoid making small talk.

8. 'Quiet leadership' is not an oxymoron.

9. Love is essential; gregariousness is optional.

10. 'In a gentle way, you can shake the world' – Mahatma Gandhi.

(Cain, 2024)

> **VIDEO**
>
> The Power of Quiet Leadership (BBC Ideas, 2020): www.bbc.co.uk/ideas/videos/the-power-of-quiet-leadership/p0929tnh
>
> In this three-minute video, Jacqueline Baxter argues that leaders don't need to be loud and confident, and makes the case for a quieter approach. She refers to Susan Cain's book.

References

Ancelotti, C with Brady, C and Forde, M (2017) *Quiet Leadership: Winning Hearts, Minds and Matches*. London: Portfolio Penguin.

Badaracco, J (2002) *Leading Quietly: An Unorthodox Guide to Doing the Right Thing*. Boston: Harvard Business School Press.

Cain, S (2012) *Quiet: The Power of Introverts in a World That Can't Stop Talking*. London: Penguin.

Cain, S (2024) The Quiet Way. [online] Available at: https://susancain.net/manifesto/ (accessed 27 February 2024).

Rock, D (2007) *Quiet Leadership: Six Steps to Transforming Performance at Work*. New York: HarperCollins.

Chapter 37: P

POSITIVE PSYCHOLOGY

For four years I was the external examiner for the MSc in Applied Positive Psychology and Coaching Psychology at the University of East London. I enjoyed reading the students' assignments, particularly when they discussed how they used some Positive Psychology Interventions (PPIs) with their practice coaching clients. I'll look at some PPIs later in the chapter.

The field of Positive Psychology has grown fast since Martin Seligman introduced the idea in his 1998 Presidential Address to the American Psychological Association. At that time, Seligman was known for his exploration of the idea of *learned helplessness* – individuals who feel they have no control over the situations they face learn to be helpless, which may result in depression or other mental illnesses. Seligman wished to stimulate the exploration of positive aspects of psychology, in contrast to the discipline's more usual concentration on mental illness and negative thinking and behaviour.

In her article 'What Is Positive Psychology, and What Is It Not?', Jessica Schrader writes:

> *Positive psychology is the scientific study of what makes life most worth living. It is a call for psychological science and practice to be as concerned with strength as with weakness; as interested in building the best things in life as in repairing the worst; and as concerned with making the lives of normal people fulfilling as with healing pathology.*
>
> (Schrader, 2008)

She adds:

> *Nowhere does this definition say or imply that psychology should ignore or dismiss the very real problems that people experience.*
>
> (Schrader, 2008)

In his book *Flourish*, Seligman (2011) sets out the PERMA framework of five elements which contribute to positive well-being and which help people to develop resilience and to thrive.

1. Positive emotions

The experience and savouring of emotions such as happiness, joy, excitement, love, pride, hope, satisfaction and gratitude contribute to psychological well-being. Integrating these into daily life can undo the harmful effects of negative emotions and can promote resilience.

2. Engagement

Being fully involved in activities that draw upon your skills and strengths, focused on the task at hand, can be immensely satisfying. Seligman (2011) called this '*being one with the music*'. This can lead to a state which Mihaly Csikszentmihalyi calls '*flow*' – when you are fully absorbed in an activity, when time seems to stop, when things feel effortless and when self-awareness seems to disappear. Engagement and flow are more likely when you are engaged in an activity that you find intrinsically rewarding and where you are utilising your top strengths.

3. Relationships

Human being are inherently social creatures. Having positive relationships – with partners, family, friends and our community – helps us to feel supported, loved and valued, and can foster positive emotions. Relationships that have a depth of understanding and respect have many benefits, in both good times and bad. Giving, receiving and sharing help to spread positivity.

4. Meaning

The search for meaning and to have a sense of value and worth is an intrinsic part of being human. Having a clear a purpose in life – having your own answer to the question *why?* – enables you to put things in context, to find meaning and to strive for goals that you desire. A sense of meaning is guided by personal values, and what gives meaning or purpose is different for everyone. You can pursue meaning in a variety of ways – for instance, through a career or a creative endeavour or a cause or a spiritual belief.

5. Accomplishments

Working towards and achieving goals, mastering a skill or completing something that you set out to do can give a sense of accomplishment. These might be small things that you put a lot of effort into, and could be individual or group-based. They might or might not be work-based successes. They can help us to have a sense of pride and achievement, and can support our feelings of well-being. Seligman (2011) suggests that achieving intrinsic goals that matter to yourself produces larger gains in well-being than external goals such as money or fame.

Strengths

A central theme in Positive Psychology is the idea of strengths. Christopher Peterson and Martin Seligman created the Values in Action Inventory of Strengths (VIA-IS) in 2004. They hoped that this would be a manual for Positive Psychology that was equivalent to the American Psychiatric Association's Diagnostic and Statistical Manual (DSM) which contains descriptions, symptoms and other criteria necessary for diagnosing mental health disorders.

The VIA-IS is a free self-assessment tool which has been completed by 27 million people. It seeks to identify an individual's profile of character strengths. The VIA website says that there is

> a common language of 24 character strengths that make up what's best about our personality. Everyone possesses all 24 character strengths in different degrees, so each person has a truly unique strengths profile.
>
> (VIA Institute on Character, 2024)

The 24 strengths are:

1. creativity;
2. curiosity;
3. judgement;
4. love of learning;
5. perspective;
6. bravery;
7. perseverance;
8. honesty;
9. zest;
10. love;
11. kindness;
12. social intelligence;
13. teamwork;
14. fairness;
15. leadership;
16. forgiveness;
17. humility;
18. prudence;
19. self-regulation;
20. appreciation of beauty and excellence;
21. gratitude;
22. hope;
23. humour;
24. spirituality.

You can complete your own assessment at www.viacharacter.org/

Positive Psychology Interventions

A notable feature of Positive Psychology over the past 25 years is the development of, literally, hundreds of Positive Psychology Interventions (PPIs). These are tools and strategies for increasing happiness and well-being, and for fostering positive emotions and thinking. The PPIs cover a wide range of themes, including:

- gratitude;
- forgiveness;
- savouring;
- strengths;
- meaning;
- humour.

Here are a couple of examples of PPIs that an individual might complete to help them to focus on positive aspects of their life. They might review them later with, for example, a counsellor or coach.

- **Three good things:** *Every night, just before going to sleep, write down three things that went well during the day.*
- **Best possible future self:** *Imagine that everything has gone the way you wanted, and all your goals have been realised. Vividly imagine this future.*

You can also use PPIs with a group of people. For example, you might adapt the above exercises to use with the team that you lead:

- **Three good things:** *Each member of the team writes down on three separate sticky notes three things that are going well in the team. Individually, they share their thoughts with the rest of the team, placing their sticky notes on a flipchart. You can then move the sticky notes around, grouping them together on themes that the team generally regard as going well.*

- **Best possible future team:** *Each member of the team draws a picture on a flipchart of what would be happening if everything in the team was going as they wanted and the team was successfully achieving their goals. (Reassure people that artistic skills don't matter here!) Each person then shares their images. A fun way to do this is the* critics' gallery *– the rest of the team try to guess what the images represent before the artist explains their picture. Then, draw out from the various pictures the key features that people generally imagine would be happening if the team was really successful.*

> **VIDEOS**
>
> Martin Seligman on Positive Psychology (Psychology Now, 2021): www.youtube.com/watch?v=G-D2kDuP-5A
>
> In this six-minute video Martin Seligman reflects on the development of Positive Psychology, noting how money doesn't produce happiness.
>
> Martin Seligman on Positive Psychology (Authentic Happiness, 2013): www.youtube.com/watch?v=faT8jw17RHE
>
> In this four-minute video Martin Seligman talks about optimism, flourishing and his hopes for the field of Positive Psychology.

References

Schrader, J (2008) What Is Positive Psychology, and What Is It Not? *Psychology Today*, 16 May. [online] Available at: www.psychologytoday.com/gb/blog/the-good-life/200805/what-is-positive-psychology-and-what-is-it-not (accessed 27 February 2024).

Seligman, M (2011) *Flourish: A Visionary New Understanding of Happiness and Well-being.* New York: Atria Books.

VIA Institute on Character (2024) The 24 Character Strengths. [online] Available at: www.viacharacter.org/character-strengths (accessed 27 February 2024).

Chapter 38: O
ORGANISATIONAL CULTURE

In an article entitled 'What Is Organizational Culture? And Why Should We Care?', Michael Watkins (2013) opens by saying:

> *If you want to provoke a vigorous debate, start a conversation on organizational culture. While there is universal agreement that (1) it exists, and (2) that it plays a crucial role in shaping behavior in organizations, there is little consensus on what organizational culture actually is, never mind how it influences behavior and whether it is something leaders can change.*

He goes on to quote a number of responses he received when he asked people on LinkedIn for their definitions.

- *Culture is how organizations 'do things'.*

- *In large part, culture is a product of compensation.*

- *Organizational culture defines a jointly shared description of an organization from within.*

- *Organizational culture is the sum of values and rituals which serve as 'glue' to integrate the members of the organization.*

- *Organizational culture is civilization in the workplace.*

- *Culture is the organization's immune system.*

- *Organizational culture [is shaped by] the main culture of the society we live in, albeit with greater emphasis on particular parts of it.*

- *It over simplifies the situation in large organizations to assume there is only one culture ... and it's risky for new leaders to ignore the sub-cultures.*

- *An organization [is] a living culture ... that can adapt to the reality as fast as possible.*

(Watkins, 2013)

He concludes his article by saying:

These perspectives provide the kind of holistic, nuanced view of organizational culture that is needed by leaders in order to truly understand their organizations – and to have any hope of changing them for the better.

(Watkins, 2013)

The best-known model of organisational culture is that of Edgar Schein. He defines organisational culture as

a pattern of shared basic assumptions that a group learns as it solves its problems of external adaptation and internal integration, which has worked well enough to be considered valid and, therefore, to be taught to new members as the correct way to perceive, think, and feel in relation to those problems.

(Schein, 1985)

His model suggests that there are three layers of organisational culture which reflect the degree to which different aspects are visible.

1. Artefacts

These are the most visible and tangible aspects of an organisation's culture; they can be recognised by people who aren't part of the culture. Examples include the layout of offices, dress code, branding and logos, policies, rituals, and office jokes. Patterns of communication or decision-making processes are behaviours than might be observed.

2. Espoused values

These represent the stated beliefs and rules of behaviour that are communicated and promoted within the organisation. They reflect the ideals and aspirations of the organisation, and may be reflected in slogans, mission statements or a statement of company values. There may be a gap between the espoused values and the actual behaviours within the organisation.

3. Basic assumptions

The deepest layer of the model are the embedded beliefs and values that are taken for granted, often go unspoken and may be unconscious. They represent the core of the organisation's culture, and may be so deeply embedded that they are hard to recognise or challenge. They nevertheless can shape individuals' thinking, decision-making and behaviour.

Schein's model suggests that the underlying basic assumptions of an organisation give rise to the espoused values, which then lead people to create the visible artefacts. Since the underlying assumptions are at the heart of the culture, changing the culture requires work at this depth. To effect successful change beyond the surface level requires identifying and shifting the shared tacit assumptions within the organisation.

Changing the culture of an organisation

In Chapter 34 on the shadow of the leader I mentioned how I was a participant in a very successful culture change programme after the formation of the gas pipeline company, Transco. The commitment of the managing director, Harry Moulson, and the expertise of the Senn Delaney facilitators were two vital elements that genuinely shifted the culture of the organisation.

In a blog called '10 Tips for Changing Your Organisation's Culture', Joe Mackintosh offers these practical ideas that resonate with my own experience of culture change in Transco.

1. **Be clear about the change you want to see.** *What are the new behaviours you want to be seeing, hearing and experiencing? ...*

2. **Make sure you have leadership commitment.** *... To create positive behaviour change, the leadership team must role model the new behaviour. ...*

3. **Get buy-in from all levels of the organisation.** *... Your employees want to make a positive difference within the organisation, but to do so they must understand and support the bigger picture.*

4. **Improve communication.** *Help individuals and teams from across the organisation to understand the change initiative with clear and consistent communication. ... If there is a culture of silence within your organisation, change initiatives are doomed from the start.*

5. **Look for positive deviants.** *There may well be some individuals or teams within your organisation who already role model the behaviour you want to see. ...*

6. **Search for opinion leaders across the organisation.** *Opinion leaders are not always managers, top performers or even the more extrovert members of staff. ...*

7. **Hold people accountable.** *Accountability is critical to the success of your culture change initiative. ...*

8. **Eliminate activities that deviate from the path to success.** *Once you have your SMART goal and understand*

the change you want to see, look for existing systems, processes and procedures which deviate from this plan and that could have a negative impact on achieving your overall behaviour change goal.

9. **Track key measures.** *Right from the outset, identify a small number of measures against which you can track progress. ...*

10. **Be consistent.** *Change cycles take time. ... Stick to your convictions and be consistent throughout the change cycle to maximise its impact and success.*

(Mackintosh, 2022)

Shaping the climate within a team

Changing the culture of an organisation requires active commitment and leadership from the top. If you are a middle or junior manager within an organisation, a more modest but practical way forward might be to seek to shift the climate within your team. Climate is about the atmosphere or mood within an organisation or a team.

In a factsheet entitled 'Organisational Climate and Culture' on the website of the Chartered Institute of Personnel and Development, Jake Young suggests that shifting the climate '*is a much more specific, tangible way to positively influence the workplace*' than seeking to change the culture of the organisation. He defines organisational climate as '*the meaning people attach to certain features of the work setting. It's the feeling or atmosphere people have in an organisation, either day-to-day or more generally*' (Young, 2023).

Young goes on to consider some important drivers that shape climate. You might reflect on how much influence you have in regard to these within, say, your department.

- **Leaders.** Leaders are essential in influencing a positive organisational climate. … [They can] shape employees' behaviour through acting as role models.

- **Team dynamics.** Creating open teams who communicate and collaborate effectively with each other is key to a positive climate. … [T]eam members need to have psychological safety – feeling they can express themselves, ask questions, share ideas and talk about mistakes without fear of punishment or judgement. …

- **Job design.** Especially important in building a climate of safety is ensuring job demands, such as workload and emotional pressures, do not outweigh the available resources. …

- **Policies, procedures and practices.** … [R]espected and lived policies and procedures can help actively shape organisational climate.

(Young, 2023)

> **VIDEO**
>
> Edgar Schein Explains Culture Fundamentals (Tim Kuppler, 2016): www.youtube.com/watch?v=gPqz315HSdg
>
> In this nine-minute video of an interview with Edgar Schein, he discusses some of the fundamentals of culture.

References

Mackintosh, J (2022) 10 Tips for Changing Your Organisation's Culture. [online] Available at: www.gra.uk.com/blog/10-tips-for-changing-your-organisations-culture (accessed 27 February 2024).

Schein, E (1985) How Culture Forms, Develops and Changes. In Kilmann, R, Saxton, M and Serpa, R (eds) *Gaining Control of the Organizational Culture*. San Francisco: Jossey-Bass.

Watkins, M (2013) What Is Organizational Culture? And Why Should We Care? *Harvard Business Review*, 15 May. [online] Available at: https://hbr.org/2013/05/what-is-organizational-culture (accessed 27 February 2024).

Young, J (2023) Organisational Climate and Culture. Chartered Institute of Personnel and Development, 12 October. [online] Available at: www.cipd.org/uk/knowledge/factsheets/organisation-culture-change-factsheet/ (accessed 27 February 2024) .

Chapter 39: N
NATIONAL CULTURE

Working at Warwick Business School affords me the privilege of meeting students from all over the globe, from many different backgrounds and cultures. I notice, for example, that students from China are much less likely to speak in class – they have come from an education system which emphasises listening to and respecting the teacher at the front of the class. If I want the Chinese students to participate actively, I can modify an exercise – for example, by sending material to be read in advance or inviting discussion in pairs or trios.

In the early 1970s, Geert Hofstede analysed the results of surveys of 116,000 IBM employees working in 50 different countries. He drew on this to identify four dimensions that distinguish one national culture from another. He later added two further dimensions.

The Hofstede Insights website offers this definition:

> *National Culture is the term we use to refer to a group of people who have been brought up within a given country. In comparison to others, these individuals tend to share certain expectations of how things should be done and values around these expectations. The expectations are usually completely formed by the age of 12 to 14 and are a product of the environment we grow up in.*
>
> (Hofstede Insights, 2023)

Since national culture differences are based on values and behaviours learnt in childhood, they are fairly stable and may take generations to change.

Here are Hofstede's six dimensions of national culture. The definitions are taken from the Hofstede Insights (2024) website.

1. **Power distance:** '[T]he extent to which the less powerful people expect and accept that power is distributed unequally.'
2. **Individualism vs. collectivism:** '*In Individualist societies people are supposed to look after themselves and their direct family only. In Collectivist societies people belong to "in groups" that take care of them in exchange for loyalty.*'
3. **Motivation towards achievement and success:** '*A high score (Decisive) indicates that the society will be driven by competition, achievement and success. … A low score (Consensus-oriented) … means that the dominant values in society are caring for others and quality of life.*' This dimension used to be termed 'Masculinity versus Femininity'.
4. **Uncertainty avoidance:** '*The extent to which the members of a culture feel threatened by ambiguous or unknown situations and have created beliefs and institutions that try to avoid these.*' A high uncertainty avoidance index indicates a low tolerance for uncertainty, ambiguity and risk-taking.
5. **Long-term vs. short-term orientation:** Societies with a culture which scores high encourage thrift and education as a way to prepare for the future. They delay short-term success in favour of success in the long term. Those which score low place a stronger emphasis on the present than the future, seeking to deliver short-term success or gratification.
6. **Indulgence vs. restraint:** '[T]he extent to which people try to control their desires and impulses. … Relatively weak control is called "Indulgence".' In a highly indulgent society, people may spend more money on luxuries and enjoy more freedom when it comes to leisure time activities. '*Relatively strong*

control is called "Restraint".' Such a society tends to suppress the gratification of needs. People are more likely to save money and focus on practical needs.

It is straightforward (and free) to download the data on different countries from Geert Hofstede's website. Here is the data for six nations.

Table 39.1 Data for six countries on Hofstede's dimensions of national culture

	Great Britain	China	USA	Germany	France	India
Power distance	35	80	40	35	68	77
Individualism	89	20	91	67	71	48
Achievement and success	66	66	62	66	43	56
Uncertainty avoidance	35	30	46	65	86	40
Long term	51	87	26	83	63	51
Indulgence	69	24	68	40	48	26

Source: http://geerthofstede.com/country-comparison-graphs/

So, for example, people in China accept much more readily than those in Great Britain that power is distributed unequally, and that duty rather than freedom is the norm. The US and Germany rate similarly in terms of achievement and success, but very differently in relation to long-term versus short-term orientation.

Erin Meyer's culture map

An alternative framework for analysing and understanding national cultures is set out by Erin Meyer in her book *The Culture Map*. Her model has eights scales.

Table 39.2 Meyer's eight dimensions of national culture

Communicating	**Low-context.** Good communication is precise, simple and clear.	**High-context.** Good communication is sophisticated, nuanced, and layered.
Evaluating	**Direct negative feedback.** Negative feedback to a colleague is provided frankly, bluntly, honestly.	**Indirect negative feedback.** Negative feedback to a colleague is provided softly, subtly, diplomatically.
Persuading	**Applications-first.** Individuals are trained to begin with a fact, statement, or opinion and later add concepts to back up or explain the conclusion as necessary.	**Principles-first.** Individuals have been trained to first develop the theory or complex concept before presenting a fact, statement, or opinion.
Leading	**Egalitarian.** The ideal distance between a boss and a subordinate is low.	**Hierarchical.** The ideal distance between a boss and a subordinate is high.
Deciding	**Consensual.** Decisions are made in groups through unanimous agreement.	**Top-down.** Decisions are made by individuals (usually the boss).

→

Table 39.2 (Continued)

Trusting	**Task-based.** Trust is built through business-related activities.	**Relationship-based.** Trust is built through sharing meals, evening drinks, and visits to the coffee machine.
Disagreeing	**Confrontational.** Disagreement and debate are positive for the team or organisation.	**Avoids confrontation.** Disagreement and debate are negative for the team or organisation.
Scheduling	**Linear-time.** Project steps are approached in a sequential fashion, completing one task before beginning the next.	**Flexible-time.** Project steps are approached in a fluid manner, changing tasks as opportunities arise.

Source: Meyer (2014)

Meyer emphasises that it is the relative positioning of different countries on any dimension, not the absolute position, that determines how people see each other. You can compare different countries on her website, although there is a modest charge for this (Meyer, E, 2024).

Awareness of the preferences of different cultures, particularly on dimensions that are very different from your own native culture, is a valuable first step in considering how to interact with others. I noted above how I modify my approach to involve students from China in lessons. I also take into account national cultural differences when I'm conducting a mediation with two people from different nationalities.

Note that these assessments of cultural differences offer a general statement about a nation. In reality, people are individuals and may not conform to a stereotype. Moreover, there may be differences within nations. I imagine that there is variation between people from California, New York City and Alabama, for example. Or from rural Scotland, inner cities in England and the leafy suburbs of London.

> **VIDEO**
>
> Erin Meyer: How Cultural Differences Affect Business (Lavin Agency, 2014): www.youtube.com/watch?v=zQvqDv4vbEg
>
> In this four-minute video Erin Meyer explains how she was stimulated to explore differences in national cultures by her experience in asking an audience in Japan if they had any questions. Her Japanese colleague knew how to read the room and identify who had a question through the *'brightness in people's eyes'*.

References

Hofstede Insights (2023) National Culture and Organisational Culture: How Are They Different and How Do They Interconnect? [online] Available at: http://news.hofstede-insights.com/news/national-culture-and-organisational-culture-how-are-they-different (accessed 27 February 2024).

Hofstede Insights (2024) Country Comparison Tool. [online] Available at: www.hofstede-insights.com/country-comparison-tool (accessed 27 February 2024).

Meyer, E (2014) *The Culture Map.* New York: PublicAffairs.

Meyer, E (2024) What is the Country Mapping Tool? [online] Available at: http://erinmeyer.com/tools/culture-map-premium/ (accessed 3 June 2024).

Chapter 40: M
MANAGING CHANGE

In Chapter 11 I looked at John Kotter's eight-step framework for leading organisational change. This is particularly relevant for the people at the top of an organisation rather than those in the middle who have to implement a change set from above. I noted that the eight steps can give a misleading impression that managing change is a linear process. In reality, managing organisational change is often messy – and often unsuccessful. A 2015 McKinsey report states: '*We know, for example, that 70 percent of change programs fail to achieve their goals, largely due to employee resistance and lack of management support*' (Ewenstein et al, 2015). And the video listed as a resource at the end of this chapter says that half of all organisational change initiatives are unsuccessful.

As the McKinsey study notes, one reason why implementing change is difficult is that the people affected often resist. I think there is a lot of truth in these words of Ronald Heifetz:

> *People love change when they know it is a good thing. No one gives back a winning lottery ticket. What people resist is not change per se, but loss. When change involves real or potential loss, people hold on to what they have and resist the change.*
>
> (Heifetz et al, 2009)

One framework that is useful for understanding loss is David Rock's SCARF model. Drawing on ideas from neuroscience, Rock

(2008) suggests that there are five factors which, when threatened, activate a fight or flight response: These are:

- Status – our relative importance to others;
- Certainty – being able to predict the future;
- Autonomy – our sense of control over events;
- Relatedness – a sense of safety with others, of friend rather than foe;
- Fairness – a perception of fair exchanges between people.

Different people value these factors differently. For example, the values of autonomy and fairness are particularly important to me personally. I am likely to react when I perceive that a proposed organisational change is going to reduce my autonomy or when it seems to be treating people unfairly. Others may resist when they feel that their status in the organisation is threatened, or when the future set-up is uncertain, or when they are concerned about losing valued relationships with colleagues or possibly clients.

I have a personal view that the most important question in change is *What does it mean for me?* I think that individuals, if they are satisfied by the answer to this question, are freed to stand back and look more objectively at the pros and cons of the change and how to play their part in its successful introduction.

Bridges' transition model

Another idea that is helpful in understanding organisational change is William Bridges' distinction between change and transition. *Change* is a shift in the externals of a situation – for example, a relocation of headquarters, a new organisational structure or the introduction of a different IT system. *Transition*, however, is psychological. Bridges (1991) writes that transition is:

> *the process that people go through as they internalize and come to terms with the details of the new situation that the change brings about. [It is] a gradual psychological process*

through which individuals and groups reorient themselves so they can function and find meaning in a changed situation.

Bridges argues that it is vital to understand and take account of psychological and emotional transition if you want to make sense of how you yourself are responding to a change or if you want to lead or support others through organisational change.

Figure 40.1 illustrates three phases of transition which people go through – the ending, the neutral zone and the beginning. Paradoxically, change starts with ending and finishes with beginning.

- In the **ending** phase, each individual involved is trying to understand what has ended and to face up to the nature of their loss. They are likely to be afraid of the unknown. It is important to appreciate that this will result in resistance. Some people may become stuck in this phase. Bridges (1991) advises that you will save yourself a lot of trouble if you remember that the *'first task of transition management is to convince people to leave home'*.
- In the **neutral** zone, the old way has ended but the new way is not established. This phase is characterised by uncertainty, disorientation, confusion and discomfort. However, Bridges suggests that in this phase there may be tremendous opportunity to create new ways of thinking and working.
- In the **beginning** phase, certainty returns. People discover new energy, new purpose and new identity. The new way of working feels comfortable, and may even seem like the only possible way.

Note that these three stages may not be sharply delineated, and different people will move forward at different paces, as illustrated in Figure 40.1.

Figure 40.1 William Bridges' transition curve

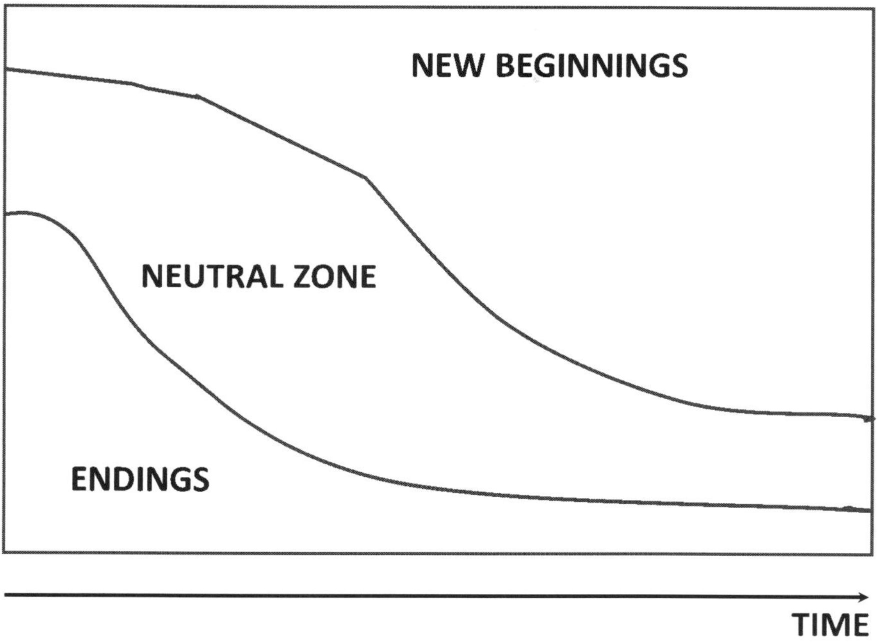

NEW BEGINNINGS

NEUTRAL ZONE

ENDINGS

TIME

Middle managers and change

In an article entitled 'From Blaming the Middle to Harnessing its Potential: Creating Change Intermediaries', Julia Balogun (2003) considers the question of whether middle managers have a negative impact on organisational change, or whether they might be a strategic asset with the potential to contribute to the success of change initiatives. She explored in depth the views of middle managers in a recently privatised UK utility company. The business was implementing strategic change in response to changing regulation and competitive threats.

She found that the middle managers were best described as *change intermediaries* who had to play four roles during the change process.

1. Keeping the business going.
2. Implementing the changes.
3. Helping others through change.
4. Undertaking personal change.

1. Keeping the business going

While the change process is unfolding, middle managers retain their responsibility for keeping the business going. For example, while there may be people being made redundant, departments have to continue delivering the outputs expected of them.

2. Implementing the changes

Middle managers also have to play their part in introducing the changes that are required – for example, by making cost reductions or improving working practices in their department. There is likely to be an ongoing tension between keeping the business going and implementing the needed changes.

3. Helping others through change

Middle managers have a responsibility to help their people cope with the changes being introduced. They might need to support people who are losing their jobs, and help others adapt to new ways of working. As noted earlier, people will be going through a process of psychological and emotional transition, needing support from their line manager. Middle managers also become role models, responsible for both formal and informal communication with their staff about the nature of the changes.

4. Undertaking personal change

Organisational change affects the roles and responsibilities of the middle managers, requiring them to interpret and carry out what is expected of them in the new set-up. They also have to look after their own well-being and, unless they are ready to retire, to find an appropriate role in the organisation or perhaps elsewhere.

Resistance to change

I noted earlier that people do not necessarily resist change, but rather they resist loss. Resistance to change may be seen as negative, something to be overcome – which indeed it often is. However, another way of viewing resistance to change is to regard it as a resource. Where there is resistance there is energy. People who resist care about something. Resistance to change may contain valuable intelligence available for a change manager who is open to feedback and prepared to listen to the views of others.

In an article entitled 'Decoding Resistance to Change', Jeffrey Ford and Laurie Ford (2009) make these suggestions for using resistance to effect productive change.

- **Explain what's changing** – don't suppress dialogue about what the change will involve.
- **Explain why** – help people understand why their jobs are being upended.
- **Look for the pitfalls** – people who voice reservations often genuinely care about getting things right, and are close enough to recognise pitfalls.
- **Elicit ideas** – using good ideas builds enthusiasm, ownership and commitment.
- **Uncover past failures** – people expect history to repeat itself, and resist going through it all over again.

> **VIDEO**
>
> 5 Critical Steps in the Change Management Process (HBS Online, 2022): https://www.youtube.com/watch?v=wxVgd8h1svU
>
> This four-minute video from Harvard Business School sets out very succinctly but in some detail five steps to plan, co-ordinate and implement change.

References

Balogun, J (2003) From Blaming the Middle to Harnessing its Potential: Creating Change Intermediaries. *British Journal of Management*, 14(1): 69–83.

Bridges, W (1991) *Managing Transitions: Making the Most of Change.* Reading, MA: Addison-Wesley.

Ewenstein, B, Smith, W and Sologar, A (2015) Changing Change Management. [online] Available at: www.mckinsey.com/featured-insights/leadership/changing-change-management (accessed 27 February 2024).

Ford, J and Ford, L (2009) Decoding Resistance to Change. *Harvard Business Review*, April. [online] Available at: https://hbr.org/2009/04/decoding-resistance-to-change (accessed 27 February 2024).

Heifetz, R, Grashow, A and Linsky, M (2009) *The Practice of Adaptive Leadership*. Boston: Harvard Business Review Press.

Rock, D (2008) Managing with the Brain in Mind. *NeuroLeadership Journal*, 1(1): 1–9.

Chapter 41: L

LISTENING

In Chapter 6 on fierce conversations I discussed four skills that are invaluable in conversations that get to the heart of the matter – listening, questioning, playing back and voicing your views clearly. Each of these skills is important when, as a manager, you seek to engage effectively with the people who work for you. They are also important more generally in meetings and in negotiating.

In this chapter I look further at listening effectively. In Chapter 6 I noted that listening is an active, attentive process. I also highlighted the difference between listening to respond and listening to understand. In the former, your focus is on what you are going to say next; in the latter your focus is on the other person and what matters to them. The former is much more common, while the latter is generally much more useful!

Figure 41.1 develops this distinction between listening to respond and listening to understand into a ladder of four levels of listening.

1. At the bottom, and it is not an uncommon experience, is *not listening at all*.
2. A second and pretty common way of listening – particularly in social situations – is *listening, waiting to speak*. This is when your focus is on what you're going to say, which probably means that you're not really paying attention to what the other person is saying.

217

3. A third way of listening – and it is typical of the kind of listening that goes on in many meetings – is *listening to disagree*. This is when you want to ensure that your view prevails. It is a selective form of listening where you are looking out for the weak points in the other person's position. It is about debate rather than dialogue, about winning or losing the argument. In some situations, this is appropriate and, indeed, essential.
4. The most powerful form of listening is *listening to understand*. This is when your focus in on seeing the world as it appears through the eyes of the other person, seeking to grasp what really matters to them. The word that is often used here is *empathy*. Note that understanding someone's perspective does not mean that you necessarily agree with it.

When you've listened to and understood the other person, it's valuable to demonstrate to them that you've understood. You might do this by playing back a reasonable accurate summary, or simply by acknowledging the strength of their sentiments.

Figure 41.1 The ladder of listening

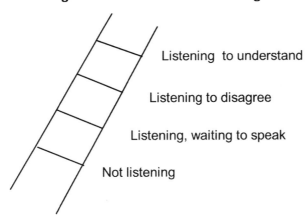

Listening with the head and listening with the heart

I also find the distinction between listening with your head and with your heart a useful pair of metaphors.

When you *listen with your head*, you concentrate on the words that the other person is saying. At a thinking level, they are communicating facts, information, arguments, ideas and concepts. You might imagine that they are communicating from their head to your head, and you may speak back from your head to their head.

However, people communicate at a feelings level too. They may vocalise their feelings – *'I'm angry'*, *'I feel sad'*, *'This is so exciting'*, etc. Often, however, the words spoken may be only the tip of the iceberg and the feelings that lie beneath the words may be expressed non-verbally – through tone of voice, or body language, or facial expression. To listen effectively you need to tune into what is not being said. You might call listening at a feelings level *listening with your heart*.

In some conversations it is entirely appropriate to listen and to respond with your head to arguments and ideas. However, to listen empathically to understand someone when they are talking about, for example, their concerns or their hopes, it is useful to listen with your heart as well as with your head. Moreover, listening to what isn't being said – and, if appropriate, encouraging the other person to express this – can be valuable.

Silence

In his book *Dialogue and the Art of Thinking Together*, William Isaacs (1999) writes of four types of silence that may be experienced in a group.

1. Awkward silences, where people feel uncomfortable.
2. Tense silences, where there is disagreement and conflict.
3. Thoughtful silences, where people are reflecting and looking inwards.
4. Sacred silences, where wisdom has replaced chatter.

Learning to be comfortable with silence can be a powerful asset. When a silence is awkward or tense, you need to consider whether and how to break the silence – perhaps with a question or a comment. When a silence is thoughtful or sacred, it's valuable to be able to sit with the silence, waiting to see what emerges. Being clear about your intention is important before you break a silence.

In her book *Fierce Conversations* Susan Scott (2002) writes of her work as an executive coach that:

> *During my conversations with the people most important to me, silence has become my favourite sound, because that is when the work is being done. Of all the tools I use during conversations and all the principles I keep in mind, silence is the most powerful of all.*

Listening creates relationship

In my work as a coach, listening to understand the other person is the fundamental conversational skill. My listening informs how I will respond – the questions I ask, the summaries I offer or the ideas I share. Similarly, as a manager, listening is a fundamental skill in the conversations you have with your team – individually or collectively.

There is a second reason why listening is so important, both in coaching and in managing people. It is captured well in this quote from Meg Wheatley (2002):

> *Why is being heard so healing? I don't know the full answer to that question, but I do know that it has something to do with the fact that listening creates relationship.*

Management, like coaching, is about a relationship. Building a relationship of rapport and trust arises from listening with respect and empathy to understand the other person.

A useful way of developing your ability to listen attentively – and to develop the relationship – is to cultivate a genuine interest in other people and their experiences – in other words, to be curious. In conversation the opposite of curiosity is certainty. When you are certain you understand the other person's point of view, you stop enquiring and you probably also stop listening.

> **VIDEO**
>
> Listening to Understand (Workplace Strategies for Mental Health, 2022): www.youtube.com/watch?v=7lphnBC3Cns
>
> This three-minute video makes a series of important points about listening to understand.

References

Isaacs, W (1999) *Dialogue and the Art of Thinking Together*. New York: Currency Doubleday.

Scott, S (2002) *Fierce Conversations*. London: Piatkus.

Wheatley, M (2002) *Turning to One Another: Simple Conversations to Restore Hope to the Future*. San Francisco: Berrett-Koehler.

Chapter 42: K

CREATING INSTITUTIONAL KNOWLEDGE

In Chapter 7 I looked at the idea of learning from experience and explored David Kolb's cycle of learning from experience. Kolb (1984) offers this definition of learning:

Learning is the process whereby knowledge is created through the transformation of experience.

In Chapter 15 I discussed two of Gareth Morgan's metaphors for an organisation – the organisation as a machine and the organisation as an organism (Morgan, 1996). One of the other metaphors that he explores is the idea of the organisation as a brain which processes information, where learning takes place and where intelligent action occurs. We might extend Kolb's definition of individual learning to produce this definition of a learning organisation:

A learning organisation is one which transforms its experience to create knowledge, and uses this knowledge to achieve or revise its goals.

Organisational memory: storing and retrieving knowledge

Learning takes place within individuals. Learning leads to knowledge, and this knowledge has to be stored and retrieved. When an individual learns, they store new knowledge in their brain or their body. They remember (and sometimes forget) what

CREATING INSTITUTIONAL KNOWLEDGE 223

they learnt, and retrieve knowledge from their memory when they need to use it. Both storage and retrieval are done by the individual.

We might ask, therefore, how does a learning organisation create, store and retrieve knowledge? How does an organisation or team develop an institutional memory?

- One way is inside individual heads. For example, an experienced accountant knows how to assess an investment proposal. A problem may arise when an individual leaves the organisation because, if the knowledge is only in their head, then it's lost to the organisation – a case of memory loss.
- A second way is to record knowledge in reports, databases, and so on. However, just because something is recorded doesn't mean that it can easily be accessed and retrieved – how many reports gather dust while someone reinvents the wheel?
- A third way is through systems and procedures. For example, a schedule of delivery routes or a budget-setting process are ways of embodying past learning in routines. There is no problem of retrieval in this case, although outdated systems may no longer be fit for purpose.
- Another way of storing information is to encapsulate learning – say, from research into new technology or from a better understanding of customer needs – in innovative products or services.
- Finally, learning can be stored through the culture of the organisation – the way we do things round here. This information is generally less tangible than that involved in routines. Acceptable behaviour, the things we talk about and the things we don't, the people regarded as role models, etc, are ways in which learning is embodied in culture. The socialisation of new recruits involves their picking up these soft elements of culture as well as the hard elements of routines and processes.

Storing and retrieving knowledge effectively is the challenge for knowledge management. The key to knowledge management in many contexts is more about relationships and communication between people than it is about systems and databases.

Four types of information

In his book *Information and Organisations* Max Boisot (1987) sets out an interesting framework to characterise different types of information. Information may be more or less easily *codified*, and information may be more or less widely *disseminated*. This leads to four types of information, which are illustrated in Figure 42.1.

Figure 42.1 Four types of information

	Low CODIFIED	High CODIFIED
DISSEMINATED High	Smell of roast beef	999
DISSEMINATED Low	Feelings towards your first boss	Your PIN number

1. The emergency telephone number, 999, is an example of a piece of information that is very clearly codified and is widely disseminated.
2. The PIN number of your bank cash card is highly codified but is only known to you. It is not widely disseminated, and this is entirely appropriate.
3. The smell of roast beef, on the other hand, is information that most of us know – it is widely disseminated. However, it is not

well codified. We would struggle to put into words or numbers what roast beef smells like.
4. You may not have thought about your first boss for many years, and may never have identified exactly what you felt about them. And perhaps no one else knows your feelings towards your first boss. Your feelings about them is information which is neither highly codified nor highly disseminated.

The skill of a wine expert lies in their ability to recognise and communicate the tastes and smells of individual wines – they can, to some extent, codify and disseminate information that is difficult to codify and disseminate.

Creating a learning organisation or team: a systematic approach

Early in my career when I was working as an economist in ICI's Mond Division, I had one of the most useful weeks ever when I attended a five-day course run by the Coverdale organisation. It was my first taste of experiential learning, and heavily influenced my future work and my approach to management development.

Recalling Kolb's idea of the experiential learning cycle, to enable your team to function as a learning organisation, you need to help them to systematically review their performance and to figure out how they want to do things differently. The Coverdale *systematic approach* is a very practical way of helping a team to review and to learn from their collective experience – that is, to translate the idea of a learning organisation into reality (Taylor, 1979).

Coverdale's systematic approach to getting things done – either as an individual or as a group – suggests that there are three stages in any task – Preparation, Action and Review.

- In the **Preparation** stage the starting point is to become very clear about the *aims*. Clarifying aims translates into crisp statements of purpose (*why are we doing this?*), deliverables

and measures of success. Having established aims, there are three activities in *planning* a piece of work – gathering information, deciding what has to be done (WHTBD) and making detailed plans.
- The **Action** stage involves carrying out the detailed plan, which may of course need to be modified as events unfold.
- The **Review** stage involves asking questions in two areas. The first concerns the results – *Did we achieve what we set out to do? How could the result be improved?* etc. The second concerns the process of how the task was done – *What went well that we can use next time? What were the difficulties and how can we avoid them next time?* etc.

The systematic approach is summarised in Figure 42.2.

Figure 42.2 The Coverdale systematic approach

```
PREPARATION

  AIMS
    o   What is the purpose of the task?
    o   What is the desired end product?
    o   How will we recognise success?

  PLANNING
    o   Information
    o   What has to be done (WHTBD)?
    o   Action plan
```

```
ACTION
    o   Carry out the plans
    o   Modify as necessary
```

```
REVIEW
    o   What did we achieve?
    o   How did we achieve it?
```

The five-day course which I attended to learn how to use the systematic approach was rolled out throughout ICI's Mond Division. When a method like this is adopted across an organisation, with genuine commitment and active involvement from the top, it offers the basis for establishing a learning organisation.

> **VIDEO**
>
> The Learning Organization (Sprouts, 2017): www.youtube.com/watch?v=4OmeQNZl3KU
>
> This four-minute video shares a number of practical ideas on how to create a learning organisation.

References

Boisot, M (1987) *Information and Organisations: The Manager as Anthropologist*. London: Fontana.

Kolb, D (1984) *Experiential Learning: Experience as the Source of Learning and Development*. Englewood Cliffs: Prentice-Hall.

Morgan, G (1996) *Images of Organization*. Thousand Oaks: Sage.

Taylor, M (1979) *Coverdale on Management*. London: Heinemann.

Chapter 43: J

JOHN ADAIR'S ACTION-CENTRED LEADERSHIP MODEL

In Chapter 18 on management as a relationship, I discussed Robert Blake and Jane Mouton's idea of the managerial grid (Blake and Mouton, 1964). They propose that, as a manager, you need to balance concern for achieving the *task* with concern for the *people* who complete the task. They emphasise that there isn't necessarily a trade-off here – an effective manager understands that the task is achieved through the efforts of the people involved.

John Adair developed his Action-Centred Leadership model independently of Blake and Mouton. He adds a third dimension in his framework for managing a group of people. Adair (1979) suggests that an effective leader needs to allocate time to:

- ensure the *task* is completed;
- keep the group or *team* working together;
- meet the *individual* needs of each team member.

Adair firmly believed that leadership was a skill which could be taught and learnt.

Completing the task

To ensure that tasks are completed effectively and efficiently, Adair says that you have to:

- specify and agree objectives;
- translate these into a plan and timeline;

- allocate resources;
- review progress and, if necessary, modify the plan;
- evaluate performance.

I think the first point is fundamental. It is vital that people are clear about what you're asking them to achieve. This seems obvious, but in many situations people are not at all clear what they are expected to deliver.

Having set the objectives or agreed them with the people involved, it is important also to monitor progress. How closely you check on the work being done by others depends on a number of factors. You may well have your own style – some people are happy to trust folk to get on with things while others must know in detail how things are progressing. Some of the people helping you may be experienced and confident, and can be left largely to get on with things. However, there may be others who are lacking in skill or commitment and so need much closer monitoring. Moreover, the importance of the task is relevant too – you may well monitor more closely a task that is crucial to the overall success of your project and be more relaxed about one which is less significant.

Keeping the team working together

To lead a team well Adair (1979) suggests that you have to:

- ensure key roles are filled by appropriate people;
- build trust and inspire teamwork;
- deal with conflict;
- expand team capabilities;
- facilitate and support team discussions and decisions.

If you are a line manager, one of the most important ways in which you invest your time is interviewing to recruit a new member of the team. Recruiting someone who isn't suitable is a mistake that you may have to live with for a very long time. On the other hand, recruiting a talented and motivated person who is going to get on well with the rest of your team is one of the delights of the role.

Managing the dynamics within the team – handling conflict, dealing with rivalries, encouraging the more reticent to contribute, putting people with complementary styles together, and so on – is also part of your role as a leader. You may, as many people do, choose to ignore tensions, disagreements and rivalries within the team. But the performance of the team and the morale of the individuals within it will be influenced by the team dynamics, and you ignore it to your cost.

From time to time, conflict or disagreement can emerge in any team. In a well-managed team conflict is acknowledged and worked through to find a way forward. In less healthy teams, conflict gets ignored, which means that it persists and undermines morale and performance.

When you are leading a group of people you may wish not only to ensure that the team is working well together to achieve their current set of objectives but you may also be seeking to build its overall effectiveness and capability. Just as individuals learn from reflecting on their experiences, so too a team collectively can learn from their performance. I looked at this in the previous chapter. One of the ways in which they can do this is to review together how things went – both the positives and the negatives – and learn from their shared experiences. When you facilitate this kind of review effectively, you can help the team to learn, to address and resolve conflict, and to build morale and team spirit.

Meeting the needs of individuals

If you are leading a group of people, Adair (1979) suggests that you have to:

- treat each member as an individual;
- acknowledge different opinions, work styles and motivation;
- encourage each individual to contribute fully;
- keep individuals informed;
- provide development opportunities according to individual needs.

One of the most important ways in which you develop effective working relationships with people is through the conversations you have with them. Many organisations have an annual performance and development review process. As I discussed in Chapter 16, this is a much richer process if it is based on regular conversations rather than an annual form-filling procedure.

In Chapter 3 I discussed coaching and mentoring. As a line manager, you can adopt a non-directive coaching approach to help people to think through how they will carry out a task, encouraging them to take ownership and responsibility. And you might at times move towards the directive end of the spectrum, drawing upon your own experience, expertise and knowledge to support and guide them – both in achieving goals and in pursuing their career and development goals.

Feedback is another important aspect of how you manage individuals. In Chapter 47 I shall explore how you can *give* constructive feedback, and also how you can help people to *generate* their own feedback on work that they have carried out.

The stance that you adopt at any point in time depends on the nature of what's happening. In a crisis, for instance, you might be focused on the task. When a group is starting a new project together, you might usefully devote time to agree how the team is going to work together. If one of your people is going through a tough time, perhaps with a loss of confidence, your focus is likely to be on that individual.

A metaphor that is useful here is to imagine that you're in a helicopter, taking an overview of everything and deciding whether the needs of task, team or individual should be your focus at that point.

> **VIDEO**
>
> Lessons in Leadership (Adair Leadership, 2019): https://adairleadership.org/
>
> The Adair Leadership website include a three-minute video where John Adair makes some key points about the Action-Centred Leadership model and about leadership more generally.

References

Adair, J (1979) *Action-Centred Leadership*. Farnborough: Gower.

Blake, R and Mouton, J (1964) *The Managerial Grid*. Houston: Gulf.

Chapter 44: I
THE INNER GAME

Tim Gallwey and the ideas set out in his book *The Inner Game of Tennis* (1975) have been hugely influential in the world of coaching. My own approach owes a great deal to the work of John Whitmore and Myles Downey, both of whom were directly influenced by Gallwey.

Gallwey was an American who was a talented tennis player in his youth, and later became an educationalist and also a tennis coach. Reflecting on how he gave tennis lessons, Gallwey realised that he was giving too many instructions and thereby causing confusion. He concluded that *'he had to teach less, so that more could be learned'* (1975). This is one of the fundamental ideas in a primarily non-directive approach to coaching.

He also noticed that in a tennis lesson the player being coached spent a lot of time talking to themselves, criticising their own performance. He postulated that within each player there were two selves – Self One who seems to give instructions to Self Two, who carries out the actions. Self One then evaluates how well or badly Self Two has performed.

Myles Downey (2003) describes Self One and Self Two as follows.

- Self One is the internalised voice of our parents, teachers and those in authority. Self One seeks to control Self Two and does not trust it. Self One is characterised by tension, fear, doubt and trying too hard.

- Self Two is the whole human being with all its potential and capacities including the 'hard-wired' capacity to learn. It is characterised by relaxed concentration, enjoyment and trust.

The outer game of tennis is the game played against the opponent on the other side of the net. Gallwey (1975) writes that the inner game is:

> *the game that takes place in the mind of the player, and it is played against such obstacles as lapses in concentration, nervousness, self-doubt and self-condemnation. In short, it is played to overcome all habits of mind which inhibit excellence in performance.*

Gallwey describes the negative thoughts of Self One as interference. It is this interference that prevents the player from performing to the level of their potential. He summarises this in the equation:

Performance = Potential − Interference

One way of reducing inner thoughts that interfere with performance is to focus attention. By focusing attention, by simply noticing what is happening, you may enter a mental state of relaxed concentration that enables you to perform at your best.

An increasingly popular approach to this is the idea of mindfulness. Mindfulness is about being fully aware of what is happening − in your mind, in your body and all around you − while it's happening. It is about attending to what is going on here and now, rather than dwelling on what occurred in the past or worrying about the future.

A key to coaching from Self Two is trust. In a later book, *The Inner Game of Work*, Gallwey (2000) wrote that:

> *Perhaps the greatest benefit the Inner Game coach brings to the conversation is to trust clients more than the clients*

> *trust themselves. And having that trust in the client can be achieved only by having learned an increasingly profound trust in oneself.*

This issue of trust seems to me to be extremely important – trust in the client, trust in yourself and trust in the coaching process.

Sometimes coaching is ineffective. Gallwey (2000) offers some words of reassurance:

> *Coaching cannot be done in a vacuum. If the learner doesn't want to learn, it doesn't make any difference if the coach is a great coach. Coaching is a dance in which the learner, not the coach, is the leader.*

The inner game of management

Let's look at how some of these ideas might translate into your role as a manager and how you support those who work for you. Reflecting on how you manage others, what are the interferences that you yourself experience that get in the way of managing well? It may be, for example, that a particular individual triggers doubt in your mind, causing you to hesitate to do what you would normally do as a manager. Or there might be particular situations or issues which make you nervous or where you lose your usual sense of yourself as a manager.

One type of doubt is the idea of *impostor syndrome*, where someone is unable to recognise their achievements, feels that any success is due to luck and is fearful of being 'found out'. They might be a perfectionist, or have a very strong *inner critic* – a harsh, judgemental, critical inner voice. They may lack confidence in their ability to be a manager – even if they've managed people very effectively for many years.

In some ways, trust is the opposite of interference. To what extent do you trust yourself to draw on your experience, intuition and concern for people to say or do what you need to say or do as a manager? If you were to trust yourself more as a manager, what might you do differently?

It may be that someone who works for you is struggling with issues of confidence or is questioning their ability or wondering if they are in the right role. You may be able to help them to tackle inner obstacles such as lack of confidence or fear of failure. You might do this through a coaching approach where you are helping them to explore their hopes and fears and to set their own direction. To what extent do you trust the individuals who work for you to know, first, what is right for them and, second, to work out how to achieve this?

Just as Gallwey notes that some clients are not ready or willing to be coached, there may be times when, despite your best endeavours, you find it impossible to manage someone effectively. If someone refuses to co-operate, to take responsibility or to perform, then you can be the greatest manager in the world and you won't be able to motivate that person.

> **RESOURCE**
>
> Inner Game of Tennis (GatesNotes, 2022): www.gatesnotes.com/The-Inner-Game-of-Tennis
>
> In this note and a two-minute video, Bill Gates discusses how valuable he found *The Inner Game of Tennis* – both as a tennis player and as a leader.

References

Downey, M (2003) *Effective Coaching: Lessons from the Coach's Coach*. London: Texere.

Gallwey, W T (1975) *The Inner Game of Tennis*. London: Jonathan Cape.

Gallwey, W T (2000) *The Inner Game of Work: Focus, Learning, Pleasure, and Mobility in the Workplace*. New York: Random House.

Chapter 45: H
HUMILITY

When you think of Donald Trump or Boris Johnson as political leaders, or Elon Musk, the CEO of Tesla, the word *humility* doesn't come to mind as one of their qualities. Arrogance, over-confidence, self-importance and perhaps narcissism seem more appropriate descriptors. All appear preoccupied with their own success, lacking empathy for others.

In his classic book *Good to Great*, Jim Collins (2001) explored the factors that enabled some companies to make the leap from good to great. One of the key factors was the presence of what he calls a level 5 leader – an executive who *'builds enduring success through a paradoxical combination of personal humility plus professional will'* (Collins, 2001). He goes on to describes someone who has personal humility as:

- demonstrating a compelling modesty, shunning public adulation; never boastful;
- acting with quiet, calm determination; relies principally on inspired standards, not inspiring charisma, to motivate;
- channelling ambition into the company, not the self; sets up successors for even more greatness in the next generation;
- looking in the mirror, not out the window, to apportion responsibility for poor results, never blaming other people, external factors or bad luck.

This humility sits alongside with *'an unwavering resolve to do whatever must be done to produce the best long-term results, no matter how difficult'* (Collins, 2001).

In an article entitled 'If Humility Is So Important, Why Are Leaders So Arrogant?', Bill Taylor (2018) offers some explanations of why so many leaders today come across as arrogant.

It may be that they believe it's not possible to be humble and ambitious at the same time. The underlying mindset here is that life is always a competition. This mindset doesn't recognise the virtues of humility.

A second reason is that, *'Humility can feel soft at a time when problems are hard; it can make leaders appear vulnerable when people are looking for answers and reassurances'* (Taylor, 2018). In reality, effective leaders know that they don't have all the answers, and that their job is to get the best ideas from others.

He concludes by saying:

> *We live in a world where ego gets attention but modesty gets results. Where arrogance makes headlines but humility makes a difference. Which means that all of us, as leaders or aspiring leaders, face questions of our own: Are we confident enough to stay humble? Are we strong enough to admit we don't have all the answers?*
>
> (Taylor, 2018)

Humility and servant leadership

I discussed servant leadership in Chapter 19. In his article 'How Humble Leadership Really Works', Dan Cable (2018) suggests that adopting the humble mindset of a servant leader is a great way to 'help people feel purposeful, motivated, and energized so that they can bring their best selves to work'. Cable (2018) writes that:

> *Humility and servant leadership do not imply that leaders have low self-esteem, or take an attitude of servility. Instead, servant leadership emphasizes that the responsibility of a*

leader is to increase the ownership, autonomy, and responsibility of followers – to encourage them to think for themselves and try out their own ideas.

He makes three suggestions on how to do this.

1. Ask how you can help employees do their own jobs better – then listen.
2. Create low-risk spaces for employees to think of new ideas.
3. Be humble.

He closes with this final sentence:

And perhaps even more important than better company results, servant leaders get to act like better human beings.
(Cable, 2018)

In another article, 'Six Principles for Developing Humility as a Leader', John Dame and Jeffrey Gedmin (2013) write that:

Humility has nothing to do with being meek, weak, or indecisive. Perhaps more surprising, it does not entail shunning publicity. Organizations need people who get marketing, including self-marketing, to flourish and prosper.

They go on to list six principles that a developing leader needs to learn.

1. *Know what you don't know.*

2. *Resist falling for your own publicity.*

3. *Never underestimate the competition.*

4. *Embrace and promote a spirit of service.*

5. *Listen, even (no, especially) to the weird ideas.*

6. *Be passionately curious.*

(Dame and Gedmin, 2013)

Humble enquiry and humble leadership

In Chapter 3 on coaching, I looked at the idea of a coaching dance where, as a manager, you move from the directive end of the spectrum, telling people what to do, to the non-directive end, asking people for their ideas. In his book *Humble Inquiry: The Gentle Art of Asking Instead of Telling*, Edgar Schein (whose classic model of organisational culture I looked at in Chapter 38) defines humble inquiry as *'the fine art of drawing someone out, of asking questions to which you do not know the answer, of building a relationship based on curiosity and interest in the other person'* (2013). He suggests that *telling*, particularly from a boss to someone who reports to them, shuts people down and makes them feel inferior. On the other hand, *asking with humility* demonstrates curiosity and an interest in the other person, which is empowering. It builds trust, promotes open communication and encourages collaboration to get things done.

In a later book, co-authored with Peter Schein, called *Humble Leadership: The Power of Relationships, Openness, and Trust* (2018), Schein sets out an approach to leadership based more on personal relationships rather than transactional role relationships. Humble leadership – relating to people as human beings – transcends hierarchical roles. It enables ideas to flow freely, mistakes to come to light quickly and adjustments to be made in real time. A personalised, co-operative relationship between leaders and followers enhances employee engagement and stimulates innovation.

> **VIDEOS**
>
> Leadership Takes Humility (Harvard Business Review, 2013): hbr.org/video/2363593483001/leadership-takes-humility
>
> In this two-minute video Tim Westergren suggests that the most effective leaders are humble.

Robert Hogan on the Importance of Humility in Leaders (Hogan Assessments, 2018): www.youtube.com/watch?v=_wQpFIctjik

In this five-minute video Robert Hogan contrasts narcissism and arrogance in leaders with humility. In his view, the best leaders are both humble and self-confident.

References

Cable, D (2018) How Humble Leadership Really Works. *Harvard Business Review*, 23 April. [online] Available at: https://hbr.org/2018/04/how-humble-leadership-really-works (accessed 27 February 2024).

Collins, J (2001) *Good to Great*. New York: HarperCollins.

Dame, J and Gedmin, J (2013) Six Principles for Developing Humility as a Leader. *Harvard Business Review*, 9 September. [online] Available at: https://hbr.org/2013/09/six-principles-for-developing (accessed 27 February 2024).

Schein, E (2013) *Humble Inquiry: The Gentle Art of Asking Instead of Telling*. Oakland: Berrett-Koehler.

Schein, E and Schein, P (2018) *Humble Leadership: The Power of Relationships, Openness, and Trust*. Oakland: Berrett-Koehler.

Taylor, B (2018) If Humility Is So Important, Why Are Leaders So Arrogant? *Harvard Business Review*, 15 October. [online] Available at: https://hbr.org/2018/10/if-humility-is-so-important-why-are-leaders-so-arrogant (accessed 27 February 2024).

Chapter 46: G

GAMES PEOPLE PLAY

In Chapter 2 I discussed a number of ideas from Transactional Analysis (TA). I noted that TA is essentially a psychodynamic approach, but one which can be used to invite people to think about their situation in perhaps a novel way and hence consider how they might behave differently. I looked at the model of ego states – Parent, Adult and Child – and of the transactions that go on between people that may create, for example, a Parent–Child relationship between a manager and someone who reports to them.

In his book *Games People Play* Eric Berne (1964) explores the idea that people play *games*. A game is a repetitive pattern of transactions between people where something is happening out of awareness at a psychological level that is different from what is taking place at a surface level and which leads to some kind of outcome or pay-off, generally but not always in the form of negative feelings or attitudes. In playing a psychological game we are following outdated strategies that we used as children to get what we needed.

When we are caught up in a psychological game, the presence of negative feelings may provide a clue that things aren't quite as they appear to be. There may be hidden meanings behind what's said, and communications aren't entirely straight.

The language used in TA is vivid – this is one reason why its ideas are engaging, but it can mean that concepts may be oversimplified and possibly misleading. TA writers often give catchy names to games. For example, in a common game called *Yes, But*, the player repeatedly seeks advice but always finds reasons not to accept it. Such a player might interact with a partner who themselves is playing the game of *Why Don't You?* in which they continually make suggestions that are rejected.

Stephen Karpman devised a framework for analysing games, the *drama triangle*. The three roles in the drama triangle are Persecutor, Victim and Rescuer. The Persecutor puts others down, while the Victim sees themselves as one down. The Rescuer also sees the Victim as one down but responds by offering help. When people play games they are in one of these three inauthentic roles, using old strategies in Parent or Child ego states rather than responding in the here and now from an Adult ego state.

Figure 46.1 The drama triangle

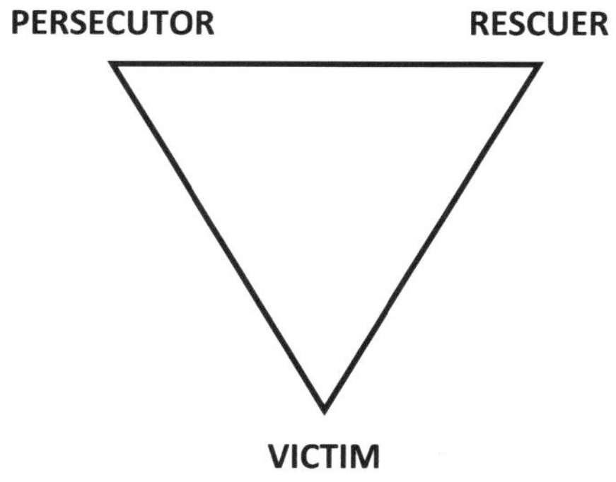

```
PERSECUTOR          RESCUER
         \        /
          \      /
           \    /
            \  /
             \/
           VICTIM
```

Source: Karpman, 1968

In the drama triangle, the Victim may seek out a Persecutor to put them down or a Rescuer to confirm their belief that they can't cope on their own. The drama triangle often involves a switch in roles as it is played out. In his article, 'The Drama Triangle – Shall We Dance?', Ian Tomlinson (2011) gives this illustration.

> Jamie: Why are you late again? You're always late for everything and I'm sick of it! (Persecutor)
>
> Lesley: I'm really sorry, I forgot to set my alarm. Please don't be mad at me. (Victim)

Jamie:	Well you're stupid and inconsiderate. I've no idea why I put up with you! (Persecutor)
Lesley:	It's not as if you are perfect. Stop shouting at me now otherwise you will regret it! (Persecutor)
Jamie:	OK, OK. Calm down. I didn't mean to upset you. (Victim)
Lesley:	Well you never help me with my lateness so what do you expect? (Persecutor)
Jamie:	OK, so from now on I will set your alarm for you and make sure you get out of the house on time. (Rescuer)

Note how the positions change, and when one player moves position that invites movement of the other player.

He goes on to ask why we play on the drama triangle:

We dance round this triangle for the same reason that we play games; we want to get our needs met but we are often too scared to ask for what we want directly. Asking for what we want, being intimate with others, feels dangerous and there is the highest risk that we may be rejected so we take one step down and play games instead to attempt to manipulate others into giving us what we want without being explicit.

(Tomlinson, 2011)

One way of dealing with game playing is to step out of the drama triangle and respond authentically from an Adult ego state or from one of the positive versions of the other ego states. The *winner's triangle*, illustrated in Figure 46.2, is an alternative to the drama triangle which recognises that people may genuinely be Vulnerable, that others really do have Power or Potency, and that helpers can be a useful Resource to support others.

Figure 46.2 The winner's triangle

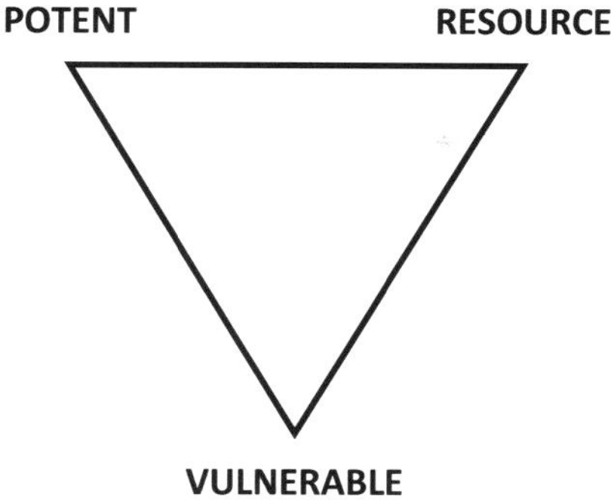

```
POTENT          RESOURCE
      \        /
       \      /
        \    /
         \  /
          \/
      VULNERABLE
```

Source: Karpman, 1968

In their chapter in *The Complete Handbook of Coaching* Trudi Newton and Rosemary Napper (2010) write that:

> *The clue to moving from game playing to authenticity is to recognize the truth behind the game roles: people do have real problems for which they have not yet learned the strategies to solve; people are genuinely and appropriately concerned about others [sic] welfare and can offer support without taking over; and people can be assertive about what they can and cannot do without 'pushing' or blaming others.*

If you are a line manager of people, then you legitimately have Power, which you need to use without slipping into a Persecutor role. And you can also be a Resource to the people who work for you without going into a Rescuer role. And anyone working in an organisation might be Vulnerable – for example, when changes in the business environment lead to job losses – without becoming a Victim.

RESOURCE

Transactions Analysis Life Positions (Lewis Psychology, 2022): www.youtube.com/watch?v=UxiWpT_SaFc

→

Another idea in TA is that of *life positions*. There are four life positions which are based on how a person sees the essential value in themselves and in others.

1. **I'm okay, you're okay.** This is a *healthy* position, where the person feels good about themselves and others, seeks to collaborate and finds it comfortable to behave assertively.
2. **I'm not okay, you're okay.** This is a *depressive* position where the person feels one down on others and tends to behave passively.
3. **I'm okay, you're not okay.** This is a *defensive* position where the person feels one up on others but behaves aggressively, competitively or insensitively to justify their stance.
4. **I'm not okay, you're not okay**. This is a *futile* position where the person considers that neither themselves nor others are any good and often feels hopeless and helpless.

In this seven-minute video Teresa Lewis explains the four positions in detail, and discusses how you might begin to shift your core life position.

References

Berne, E (1964) *Games People Play: The Psychology of Human Relationships*. New York: Ballantine Books.

Karpman, S (1968) Fairy Tales and Script Drama Analysis. *Transactional Analysis Bulletin*, 7(26): 39–43.

Newton, T and Napper, R (2010) Transactional Analysis and Coaching. In Cox, E, Bachkirova, T and Clutterbuck, D (eds) *The Complete Handbook of Coaching*. London: Sage.

Tomlinson, I (2011) The Drama Triangle – Shall We Dance? [online] Available at: https://manchesterpsychotherapy.co.uk/the-drama-triangle-shall-we-dance/ (accessed 27 February 2024).

Chapter 47: F

GIVING, GENERATING AND GATHERING FEEDBACK

One of the key responsibilities of a manager is to give feedback to the people who report to them. Relevant, accurate feedback can enable someone to perform more effectively and deliver better results. It can also support them in their development, helping them to build on strengths or to address weaknesses. And feedback that is discussed and explored can enhance the quality of the relationship between the two people concerned. Feedback releases potential.

Giving feedback

There are times when it is particularly important to give feedback. For example, you may wish to support and encourage someone who is new to a role or perhaps lacking in confidence.

Alternatively, it might be that someone is underperforming and is unwilling to face up to or take responsibility for their behaviour. In this situation, it is essential that you tell them what you think about their performance or their behaviour, inviting them to discuss this. You may find that you need to state clearly and specifically, with supporting evidence, what the person is doing wrong.

Many managers find it very difficult to give feedback to others. There are a number of reasons why this might be so. It may be because the manager – and perhaps also the person receiving the feedback – feels uncomfortable about engaging in this kind of conversation, particularly if the feedback is seen as negative.

In Chapter 6 I discussed how to have a conversation that gets to the heart of a matter. It could be that the manager doesn't have a clear idea of what would constitute effective behaviour and so is unable to offer constructive feedback. Or perceived lack of time may be used as an excuse.

It is very helpful if feedback is specific. Imagine that I've just given a presentation. Here are three examples of feedback I might receive.

1. I really liked your slides.
2. I didn't think your slides were very good.
3. The font size on your slides was small, which meant that the people at the back of the room couldn't read them.

Only the third piece of feedback is useful. It is specific, it is relevant, it states the effect of my action and I can do something to correct matters.

When giving feedback it is worth checking internally what your intent is before you start to speak. If you simply want to vent your feelings of frustration or disappointment, then be clear that this is what you are doing. If your intent is genuinely to help the other person to be more effective next time, then consider carefully what you are going to say. Giving feedback that the other person doesn't hear or accept may release some of your emotions but is unlikely to make any difference to their performance.

The idea of *feedforward* is a useful variation of feedback. The aim is to offer someone an idea on what they might usefully do differently in future. Here is a simple illustration building on the above example.

4. Your slides would have more impact if the font size was larger.

In the same way that a manager might find it difficult to give feedback, so too some people find it hard to receive feedback. They might feel anxious or that they are being criticised, and they may become defensive. It is much more useful if they are open to, at least, hearing the feedback that's being offered. Rather than offering excuses to justify what they did, it's more valuable to listen in order to understand. And, as I've noted elsewhere, listening to understand does not mean that you agree. It can be helpful too to ask when anything isn't clear. A feedback session is an opportunity to clear misunderstandings and, perhaps, to start afresh. Accurate, relevant feedback provides an opportunity to improve both performance and relationships.

Generating feedback

In Chapter 3 I looked at the idea of a coaching dance where a manager moves skilfully between telling and asking. An alternative to *giving* feedback is *generating* feedback. The aim is to encourage the other person to construct their own feedback on their performance. When someone generates their own feedback, they will be more aware of what they did and more likely to take responsibility for performing differently.

Here are some illustrative questions that you might choose from to help someone to generate feedback for themselves after they've completed a piece of work. Note that they are open questions that encourage exploration.

- What were you pleased about in this piece of work?
- What were you less pleased about?
- On a scale of 1 to 10, how satisfied were you? What would have made it one point higher?
- What would you do differently next time?
- What have you learnt from doing this project?

If after reviewing a piece of work they are still missing something important, it's valuable to point this out. You may find that there is no need for you to add anything because they have identified all of the key points themselves.

Gathering feedback

Beyond giving and generating feedback, there is also the idea of *gathering* feedback, where you set out deliberately to collect information that will enhance your performance or your development. If you wish to do this, begin by identifying who is well informed about your work and is likely to share their views honestly with you. You can then invite them to respond – either in conversation or in writing – to some open questions on how they regard your attitude, behaviour or performance. A variation of this is to ask someone – such as a learning and development specialist – to gather this feedback on your behalf and then to take you through it in a coaching conversation.

A common way of gathering feedback is to take part in a 360-degree feedback exercise. This collects feedback from people all around yourself – your own manager, peers, reports and possibly customers or clients. It's useful too to complete a similar questionnaire on yourself, enabling you to compare your self-assessment with those of others. It may be that your organisation has its own 360-degree feedback tool, perhaps based on its values or competences.

When I worked in management development, I often took people through their 360-degree feedback report. While comparing their 'scores' with how others had rated them on specific attributes was useful, generally the most valuable part of the feedback were the verbatim comments on strengths and weaknesses (or on *should do more of* and *should do less of*) from respondents. While the comments were not attributed to any one individual, the recipient often had a view on who was likely to have said what.

VIDEO

Giving Feedback Effectively (Primeast, 2016): https://primeast.com/us/insights/mastering-communication/Giving-Feedback-Effectively

This five-minute video and the text below it discusses a number of important aspects of giving feedback effectively, summarising these in a series of bullet points. For example, it suggests this three-part process for giving feedback to someone.

1. Capture the situation.
2. Describe the behaviour.
3. Describe the impact.

It also includes these points on how to receive feedback.

- Listen attentively.
- Repeat only what you heard (to clarify).
- Ask for specifics (what you are doing well, what you are doing not so well).
- Show appreciation by saying 'thank you'.
- Ask if (and when) you can check back.

Chapter 48: E

HANDLING EMAILS

As you begin to read this chapter, you might take a look at what is on the top of your desk. Is it neat and tidy, or is it strewn with papers and materials for a variety of things you're working on at the moment? In his book *Clear Your Desk,* Declan Treacy (1998) advises that you should only have on your desk the papers that relate to the task you are currently doing. When you are ready to move on to the next task, put those papers in your filing system and bring out the papers for the new task. Otherwise, if you have papers relating to different jobs visible on top of your desk, you will from time to time pick up unrelated paperwork, spend some time looking at it but not make any decisions. In this way you will waste several minutes and divert your attention from what you meant to work on. Over the course of a day – or a year – you'll waste lots of time and continually lose focus. So, Treacy recommends, clear your desk!

I've adapted Treacy's idea of clearing your desk to help me manage my emails. You might call this *Clear your inbox*. There are only four things you can do with an email.

1. Delete it.
2. Reply to it.
3. Forward it.
4. File it – and put it on your *To do* list.

Let's look at these four possibilities in turn.

1. Many emails – spam is the obvious but not the only example – don't require you to do anything. Delete them straight away.

2. Some emails require a quick reply which may take you seconds or perhaps a few minutes. Reply to them now. File if necessary.
3. Other emails require a response from someone else. Forward the email to the appropriate person or people, passing on the task. File if necessary.
4. Some emails create work for you. One of the features of emails is that two lines of text might generate months of work. Or, there might be an attachment that you want to read carefully. You can't fully deal with such an email now. Put it on your *To do* list – my own practice is to mark the email with a red flag, which means it's shown in the *For Follow Up* folder in Outlook. You will have to return to this email – perhaps many times – so file it in a folder where you will be able to find it easily whenever you need to look at it.

If you adopt this practice, then you can clear your inbox. You'll find this is far more effective than having an inbox full of dozens or even hundreds of emails that you may or may not have opened but not dealt with – alongside all the new emails that have arrived since you last looked. And you won't waste time glancing guiltily at all those emails that do need attention at some point.

To make this approach work, you need a suitable filing system for your email account. Taking some time to set up an email filing system that works for you is a useful investment of time that will save far more time in the long run.

I also find that it's useful to clear my *Sent* folder several times a day. I reckon that at least three quarters of the emails I send don't need filing and so can be deleted. I know where to file my replies as I've just been working on them. I can then easily retrieve these emails later if necessary. I also look at my *Junk* folder every day, deleting the 99 per cent that are irrelevant but spotting the odd one that I do want to read.

One suggestion for managing the time you spend on emails is to deal with them at specific times rather than continually through the day. Depending on the nature of your role, this might be one or more times a day, and certain times of the day will suit you better than others. And I suggest that you silence the noise and disable the pop up that tells you a new email has arrived, diverting you from the task that you're currently engaged on.

Note that clearing your inbox in this way doesn't stop the emails arriving in the first place. That's a different problem! To tackle this might require you to step back and clarify which parts of your role are central and which parts you might withdraw from or pass on to others. This could be a significant and strategic review, one which you need to take care over. But there might be some quick wins – for example, do you really need to be on the distribution list for the agenda and minutes of that meeting you never attend?

One of the consequences of how we adjusted to remote and hybrid working during and after the pandemic was the adoption of Teams or Zoom for many meetings. I personally find that this enables me to work very efficiently from home several days a week – which means I don't have to drive to and from work on those days. The University of Warwick, where I work, adopted Teams as its preferred approach. This now means that I often receive messages on Teams rather than by email. I haven't quite worked out how to adjust to this – but I do find it a little frustrating having electronic correspondence through two completely different media.

One final thought on handling emails concerns the times when you receive an email that 'pushes your button', causing you to feel frustrated or angry. You might be tempted to dash off an immediate reply. Don't – you may well seriously regret the consequences of sending an email that you wrote in the heat of the moment. One way of releasing some of the tension you feel is to write the email but don't send it. Have a look at it the next day – you can then edit it to be a more constructive response, or you might not send it at all. If you are drafting such an immediate emotionally charged reply, make sure you don't have anyone in the address list in case you accidentally hit the *Send* button.

> **VIDEOS**
>
> How to Write Better Emails at Work (Jeff Su, 2021): hbr.org/2021/08/how-to-write-better-emails-at-work
>
> In this seven-minute video, which has the transcript attached, Jeff Su shares a number of practical tips on how to write better emails at work. I particularly like his fourth point – state your main point first in an email, followed by necessary context – rather than giving a lot of information before you get to what you want to say or ask for.
>
> Email Etiquette Tips (Adriana Girdler, 2018): www.youtube.com/watch?v=ol3rVQFye9w
>
> In this six-minute video Adriana Girdler offers practical suggestions on email etiquette and on how to write emails that are more likely to be noticed and acted upon. She notes that there are times when it's better to, for example, pick up the phone rather than send an email.

Reference

Treacy, D (1998) *Clear Your Desk*. London: Arrow Business.

Chapter 49: D

DECISION-MAKING

One of the key things which a manager needs to do is to make decisions. There may be situations where what needs to be done is obvious – here it's easy to make the decision. There may be times when the situation is complex and it's not at all clear what has to be done – it might be a real challenge to make a good decision. There may also be times when the right decision is going to have significant, negative implications for the people affected – it may be tempting to defer or even avoid making the necessary decision.

The website of Lucidchart, a web-based diagramming application, offers this apparently simple seven-step structure for making and reviewing a decision.

1. *Identify the decision.*
2. *Gather relevant information.*
3. *Identify the alternatives.*
4. *Weigh the evidence.*
5. *Choose among the alternatives.*
6. *Take action.*
7. *Review your decision.*

(Lucidchart, nd)

This is a clear process which might be a useful framework in many situations. The logic behind the model makes sense – and seems to miss the point that the world often isn't as clear and rational as is implied. In his article 'How to Make Great Decisions, Quickly', Martin Moore (2022) offers a more nuanced framework of eight *'core elements of great decisions'*.

1. Great decisions are shaped by consideration of many different viewpoints.

2. Great decisions are made as close as possible to the action.

3. Great decisions address the root cause, not just the symptoms.

4. Great decisions are made by a clearly accountable person.

5. Great decisions consider the holistic impacts of a problem.

6. Great decisions balance short-term and long-term value.

7. Great decisions are communicated well to stakeholders.

8. Great decisions are timely.

(Moore, 2022)

In his article 'What Makes an Effective Executive', Peter Drucker (2004) writes that:

A decision has not been made until people know:

- *the name of the person responsible for carrying it out;*
- *the deadline;*

- *the names of the people who will be affected by the decision and therefore have to know about, understand and approve it – or at least not be strongly opposed to it; and*
- *the names of the people who have to be informed of the decision, even if they are not directly affected by it.*

Optimising or satisficing

Classical economics suggests that individuals and organisations rationally seek to make decisions that *optimise* a situation – for instance, they may wish to maximise profits or minimise costs. Herbert Simon (1955), who won the Nobel Prize for Economics, suggests that people make decisions by *satisficing* (a combination of 'satisfy' and 'suffice') rather than optimising. Satisficing is a decision-making strategy that aims for a satisfactory or adequate result, rather than the optimal solution.

Simon argued that people cannot obtain or process all of the information needed to make a fully rational decision. Moreover, they often need to consider the interests of others, and there may also be political factors that have to be taken into account. He termed these cognitive and social limits – and the way in which they shape decision-making – *bounded rationality*.

David Kantor's three languages

David Kantor has a very interesting model that is relevant to how people make – or don't make – decisions. In his book *Reading the Room* (2012), he suggests that each of us speaks in one of three preferred languages.

1. People who speak the language of **Power** focus on making decisions and agreeing actions.
2. Some individuals speak the language of **Meaning** and attend to ideas and ways of understanding.

3. Those who speak the language of **Affect** concentrate on feelings and on connections between people.

At the risk of stereotyping people, the engineers I met when I worked in the gas pipeline company, Transco, spoke the language of Power – they wanted clear decisions and enjoyed taking action. The academics I've met since joining the University of Warwick speak the language of Meaning – they can debate ideas endlessly without ever committing to taking action. I imagine that a group of counsellors or social workers might speak the language of Affect, focusing on the human aspects of a situation.

Kantor (2012) suggests that people who speak these different languages have problems in understanding one another akin to, for example, people whose native tongue is French, Russian or Japanese. I think that my own 'native tongue' is the language of Meaning. I believe that a career in organisations has helped me to become fairly fluent in the language of Power, while my work as a coach has developed my ability to use the language of Affect. You might like to consider how well you speak each of Kantor's three languages.

Dimensions of the Myers–Briggs Type Indicator

In Chapter 10 I considered the four dimensions of the MBTI. Some of these are relevant to how people make decisions. The third dimension of the MBTI is specifically about this. Those with a Thinking or T preference use logic and analysis to guide them. They take a detached standpoint and apply objective criteria, rules or principles when making a decision. On the other hand, people with a Feeling or F preference base their decisions on their values and convictions. They are concerned about how a decision will impact on people. They are more likely to base a decision on fairness rather than consistency.

The second dimension of the MBTI refers to how people prefer to take in information and what kind of information they like to pay attention to. People with a Sensing preference like to see the detail and want information to be precise and accurate. And someone with an Intuition preference may be happy with the big picture only, and may get bored if you give them too much detail.

In regard to the fourth dimension of the MBTI, people with a Judging preference like to make plans with milestones and deadlines. Those with a Perceiving preference feel constrained by plans, and dislike making a decision until they have to.

You might like to reflect upon how you yourself like to take in information, take decisions and make (or don't make) plans.

> **VIDEO**
>
> Bounded Rationality (Tutor2U, 2021): www.tutor2u.net/economics/reference/behavioural-economics-bounded-rationality
>
> In this short video Geoff Riley discusses bounded rationality and satisficing. He emphasises that *'bounded rationality is not the same as irrationality, because decision-makers are still attempting to make as rational a decision as possible'*.

References

Drucker, P F (2004) What Makes an Effective Executive. *Harvard Business Review*, June. [online] Available at: https://hbr.org/2004/06/what-makes-an-effective-executive (accessed 27 February 2024).

Kantor, D (2012) *Reading the Room: Group Dynamics for Coaches and Leaders*. San Francisco: Jossey-Bass.

Lucidchart (nd) 7 Steps of the Decision-Making Process. [online] Available at: www.lucidchart.com/blog/decision-making-process-steps (accessed 27 February 2024).

Moore, M G (2022) How to Make Great Decisions, Quickly. *Harvard Business Review*, 22 March. [online] Available at: https://hbr.org/2022/03/how-to-make-great-decisions-quickly (accessed 27 February 2024).

Simon, H (1955) A Behavioral Model of Rational Choice. *The Quarterly Journal of Economics*, 69(1): 99–118.

Chapter 50: C
CONFIDENCE

In my work as a coach, one of the hardest challenges is to help a client whose lack of confidence prevents them from pursuing their goals and aspirations. Issues of confidence or low self-esteem can run very deep within a person. For some, their lack of confidence may be so profoundly ingrained that it may require referral to a therapist or counsellor to help them address this. As a coach, I must work within appropriate boundaries – I'm not a qualified counsellor. However, I can draw on ideas from cognitive behavioural coaching or solution-focused coaching to help someone to think differently about their situation and to behave more effectively.

A cognitive behavioural approach

As a line manager, you might similarly help someone who works for you to explore and, hopefully, modify their lack of confidence by inviting them to consider how they think of themselves or their situation. Note that you need to take care and not probe too deeply. The key idea that is central to a cognitive behavioural approach can be summarised in the words of the ancient Stoic philosopher, Epictetus, who said that, '*People are disturbed not by things, but by the views which they take of them*'.

One technique is the use of the ABCDE model to dispute self-limiting thoughts and beliefs.

- A Activating event.
- B Beliefs and perceptions about this event.

C Consequences – cognitive, emotional, behavioural, physical or interpersonal.
D Disputing of self-limiting beliefs.
E Effective and new ways of thinking and behaving.

Here is a simple illustration. Imagine that one of your team is due to deliver a presentation next week – this is the activating event (A). In anticipation, they are starting to panic, and find that they can't sleep or eat properly – these are the emotional and behavioural consequences (C).

Now if A really did cause C, then everyone who had to do a presentation next week would have similar symptoms. Rather, it's not A that causes C directly but rather it is the mental processing of A via the person's belief system, B, which leads to C. By disputing (D) unhelpful beliefs, the individual may be enabled to develop more effective (E) ways of thinking and behaving.

An unhelpful belief in this context might be: *If someone asks me a question that I can't answer, then I'll look foolish and my reputation will be ruined.*

An alternative view might be: *I know a lot about this subject. I will prepare thoroughly. If there is a question I can't answer, then I'll promise to check it out and get back to the questioner.*

You might consider using the ABCDE model to help one of your team to think – and act – differently about an upcoming challenge that they feel anxious about.

Reframing

Helping someone to view things differently might be termed *reframing*. In *The Coach's Coach*, Alison Hardingham (2004) writes that, '*Reframing is changing the meaning of something by putting it in a different context. ... Often, when we are stuck, a reframe will help us move forward*'.

Here is an example of a simple reframing question: *So far we've been talking about the difficulties you may face in the new role. What opportunities might it also offer?*

In Chapter 2 I looked at the idea from Transactional Analysis (TA) of Parent, Child and Adult ego states, noting how people might find themselves in an Adapted Child ego state where they replay attitudes and behaviours they learnt as a child in order to comply with the demands of others. I also noted that being in an Adult ego state – present in the here-and-now, aware of your thoughts and feelings, and focused on the task in front of you – is usually a much more effective ego state. You might use this (deceptively) simple framework to help someone lacking in confidence to consider what state of mind they wish to be in when preparing for and participating in a situation they find challenging – such as making a presentation or taking part in an important meeting.

A solution-focused approach

Another approach to coaching which overlaps with a cognitive behavioural approach is known as solution-focused coaching. As the name suggests, this focuses on solutions rather than problems. While the past or present might be explored, the conversation is more about the future, with an emphasis on action, on clear goals and on positive change.

It is also about tapping into the ideas, expertise and resources of the other person. For example, it may be that the individual does behave confidently and effectively in some situations – they may be able to draw on this to enable them to perform well in the context that is troubling them. As an illustration, I recall a coaching session with someone who was nervous about an upcoming presentation. She actually took part in some high-quality amateur dramatic performances, sometimes singing solo on stage. She was able to draw on these experiences to help her approach the presentation in a more confident frame of mind.

One technique that can also be useful here is to help the person identify an *anchor*. This is simply a stimulus that enables them to access a resourceful state that will help them to perform well. In the previous example, I asked the client to recall words or images or simple physical actions that they associated with going on stage. They were able to anchor this confident state with the action of clasping their hands together and saying to themselves the phrase *I'm good at this.* They could draw upon this whenever they began to deliver a presentation.

A cycle of development

It may be the case that the person lacks confidence because they've not had the necessary experience to face a new challenge. In Chapter 7 I considered how a manager can support the development of their people by offering them appropriately challenging experiences and helping to reflect upon and learn from these experiences. I might extend the cycle of learning from experience, which I presented in Figure 7.1, to the cycle of development shown in Figure 50.1. As the individual succeeds in meeting a challenge, their sense of their capability and their confidence grow. They can begin to aim higher, taking on bigger tasks and roles.

Figure 50.1 A cycle of development

Manager offers a challenging experience

Individual is ready to take on greater challenges   Individual successfully tackles the challenge

Individual's confidence and sense of self grows.   Manager helps the individual to articulate what they did well and what they can improve upon

This is like a pattern found by John Kotter among successful general managers, which he calls the *success syndrome*. He writes of these managers that:

> They did well in an early assignment; that led to a promotion, or a somewhat more challenging assignment; that reinforced (or even increased) their self-esteem and motivation and led to an increase in their formal or informal power and an increase in the opportunities available to develop more power. More challenging jobs also stretched them and helped build their skills.
>
> (Kotter, 1982)

VIDEO

Build Your Self-Confidence (MindTools Videos, 2018): www.youtube.com/watch?v=Edor4D-zAkg

This short video offers a number of ideas on how to build your own self-confidence.

References

Hardingham, A (2004) *The Coach's Coach*. London: Chartered Institute of Personnel and Development.

Kotter J (1982) *The General Managers*. New York: Free Press.

Chapter 51: B
BUSINESS SCHOOLS

In September 2013 I began working as a Professor of Practice at Warwick Business School (WBS). This was a generic role – WBS wanted to recruit people who had practical experience working in organisations. I went to meet the Dean, Mark Taylor, to ask him what he wanted me to do. He replied – with an apology for using the term – *'soft skills'*. This led me to create a very distinctive core module on our full-time MBA, LeadershipPlus. With an emphasis on experiential learning, the module aims to help each student to learn about themselves, about collaborating effectively in a group and about identifying their personal approach to managing and leading people. The module gets great feedback from most students, while a few, who would prefer a more traditional academic approach, don't enjoy it. We know from discussions with prospective students that it is a great asset in recruiting people to the full-time MBA.

The content of this book is about these *soft skills* – understanding and managing yourself, working in teams and managing other human beings. The other modules on the full-time MBA at WBS help students to learn what we might term *hard skills* – such as finance, strategy, marketing, operations management and entrepreneurship. They are also encouraged to explore issues of sustainability and corporate social responsibility.

As a manager progresses to more senior roles in organisations, they need to develop a working understanding of these topics – to develop their hard skills. All organisations – whether they are in the commercial, public or charity sectors – require money to operate. While there will be accountants and other support staff in the finance department, as a manager you need to be able to read and understand financial statements. You may not need to be an expert in analysing detailed company accounts, but you do need to understand, for example, sales and cash flow projections for the product or area you are working in. You may need to learn how to make or assess a business case which is asking for an investment of funds, and understand how your organisation measures rate of return.

As I noted at the start of Chapter 31, the word *strategy* derives from the Greek word *strategos*, which means a general. To act strategically requires you to stand back from the detail, to be clear about the overall aim and to create a plan of action to pursue this. It also requires you to review and modify the strategy as events unfold – in the words of a military maxim (articulated by the German field marshal, Helmuth von Moltke), '*No plan survives contact with the enemy*'. The heavyweight boxer Mike Tyson expressed the same idea when he said, '*Everyone has a plan until they get punched in the mouth*'. While the strategy of an organisation generally is set from the top, at any level it's possible to think strategically about what you're trying to achieve in the team that you lead or in the role that you carry out. In Chapter 14 I looked at the value of being able to say *no* in order to concentrate on what's most important and to manage your time effectively. It's also valuable to think strategically about your own career, your development and your work–life balance.

You can also draw upon ideas from marketing to manage yourself and your team even if you have no direct involvement in the commercial activities of your organisation. The Chartered Institute of Marketing offers this definition:

> *Marketing is the management process responsible for identifying, anticipating and satisfying customer requirements profitably.*

> It is about understanding the competitive marketplace and ensuring you can tap into key trends, reaching consumers with the right product at the right price, place and time.
> (Chartered Institute of Marketing, 2023)

Whatever function you work in, engaging effectively with the internal clients who use the services that your team offers will enable you to keep your offering up to date and relevant. You might also take initiatives to create awareness of and generate interest in the services you offer, particularly if you are establishing new ones. It may well be that no money ever changes hands, but you consciously take steps to ensure that you and your team continue to provide a first-class, relevant service. Finally, on a personal level, you might ensure that you market yourself and your capabilities well to support your own development and progression within your career.

Critical Issues in management

Another key part of the teaching that I do at Warwick Business School is to act as a seminar tutor on a final year undergraduate module called Critical Issues in Management. It is again a distinctive module, based entirely on case studies which students analyse in syndicates and then make presentations on to their wider seminar group. The welcome page for the module begins:

> The ability to think critically is an increasingly important attribute. It is only by thinking critically that we can hope to make a positive impact, whether this is in our own lives, in organizations, or in wider society. Thinking critically demands curiosity, openness, and a propensity to consider issues from different perspectives.

The case studies invite the students to explore and research complex problems with no 'right answer'. They are encouraged to balance appreciation of the local detail of a case with a wider consideration of the 'big picture'. We expect them to make clear reasoned judgements and recommendations based on weighing evidence. We also expect them to note limitations of any theory they use and of any recommendations they make.

We hope that the module helps each student to prepare for their future roles as managers. The ability to thinking critically is an important skill for any manager, particularly in today's volatile, uncertain, complex and ambiguous (VUCA) business environment.

> **RESOURCES AND VIDEO**
>
> If you'd like to learn more about the topics mentioned above, but don't have the time to study for an MBA, there is a book called *MBA in a Day* by Steven Stralser (2016). And, if you have a bit more time, you might be interested in *The 10-Day MBA* by Steven Silbiger (2010). I haven't actually read either of these – I'm not necessarily recommending them. I guess if the books really did deliver what they promise, I'd be out of a job!
>
> MBA in a Day (Steven Stralser, 2007): www.youtube.com/watch?v=MeyhbmnrU7w
>
> In this four-minute video Steven Stralser advertises his *MBA in a Day*, which is structured around four modules on People, Money, Markets, and Systems & Planning.

References

Chartered Institute of Marketing (2023) What Is Marketing? [online] Available at: www.cim.co.uk/content-hub/quick-read/what-is-marketing/ (accessed 27 February 2024).

Silbiger, S (2010) *The 10-Day MBA: A Step-by-Step Guide to Mastering the Skills Taught in Top Business Schools*. London: Piatkus.

Stralser, S (2016) *MBA in a Day 2.0: What You Would Learn at Top-tier Business Schools (If You Only Had the Time!)*. Rochester: The Center for Professional Development.

Chapter 52: A
ASSERTIVENESS

The ability to behave assertively is a vital skill in both everyday life and in managing people. It enables you to communicate clearly what you want or need, which can help you to influence others, to negotiate well and perhaps to become more confident.

Assertiveness is about balancing your needs with the rights, needs and wants of others. It is being able to state clearly your own position while, at the same time, having empathy and regard for the view of others. In seeking to get things done, an assertive manager treats people fairly and respectfully. In turn, they are likely to be respected by their team and seen as someone that people wish to work for.

Here is a definition of what I like to call *genuine assertiveness*:

> *Assertiveness is the ability to state clearly and confidently what you want or need in a situation* and *to allow the other party to state clearly what they want.*

In everyday language, when someone describes another person as assertive, they often mean that he or she is good at getting their own way. They pursue their own interests without regard for others, and may come across as pushy or even bullying. This might be termed *basic assertiveness*. It could also be called aggressiveness.

Basic assertiveness is like a one-way street. Genuine assertiveness is a two-way street. Figure 52.1 distinguishes genuine assertiveness with being passive, on the one hand, and aggressive, on the other.

Figure 52.1 Assertive, aggressive and passive stances

In Chapter 25 I looked at the Thomas–Kilmann framework of five ways of handling conflict, which I defined as any form of disagreement, no matter how large or small. Behaving assertively is essential if you wish to collaborate with the other person to create a win–win outcome. If you behave passively, your needs won't be met – you avoid the conflict or accommodate the wishes of the other person. Behaving aggressively means that you are only interested in achieving what you want – in other words, you compete to win.

Another pattern of behaviour is termed passive-aggressive. This may be when someone disagrees covertly but, rather than stating clearly their views, they make subtle digs or negative comments. It's easier to deal with someone who openly disagrees than with someone who – metaphorically or literally – rolls their eyes when you're speaking.

Rights and responsibilities

A useful idea in assertiveness is the notion of *rights*. People who find it hard to be assertive often do not recognise the rights which they are entitled to. For example, each of us has is the right to say *no*. However, as well as rights, we also have *responsibilities*.

When you say *no*, you need to be prepared to accept the consequences. It may be okay to say *no* to a request to work late because you have something important going on that evening. But if you are never prepared to say *yes* to a reasonable request to work late, then you may acquire a reputation for being selfish or uncommitted or not a team player. Moreover, while you have the right to say *no*, there may be times when it's wise to say *yes* even if you'd rather say *no*.

In *The Assertiveness Pocketbook*, Max Eggert (2011) gives examples of rights that each of us has – alongside an equivalent responsibility when we are acting with genuine assertiveness, as shown in Table 52.1.

Table 52.1 Rights and responsibilities

Right	Responsibility
Be treated with respect	Respect the rights of others
Express opinions and feelings	Welcome the opinions and feelings of others
Set your own goals	Help others to work towards their goals and objectives
Refuse a request or say *no*	Encourage others to use their time in the way that they want
Ask for what you want	Encourage others to fulfil their needs

Eggert, 2011

Speaking assertively

In Chapter 6, I discussed how to have a fierce conversation – that is, one which gets to the heart of the matter and explores different perspectives. I noted the importance of the conversational skill of voicing – that is, the ability to state clearly what you think and the reasons that underlie your thinking. This ability to voice is at the heart of communicating assertively.

There are two things which often make a statement more assertive. The first is to explain the reasons behind your views or to state why something is important to you. The second — which may not be appropriate in some settings — is to state how you feel about a situation. To illustrate these points, compare the following statements.

- I won't be able to attend the meeting.
- I won't be able to attend the meeting because I have a hospital appointment.
- I can't talk to you now.
- I can't talk to you now because I'm very upset.

Another point which is very helpful in speaking assertively is to make sure that you don't dilute your message. It is really useful to make a simple, crisp statement, setting out your view or asking simply and directly for what you want. However, adding lots of detail, explanation or justification usually weakens the impact of the statement. So too does adding an unnecessary apology or putting yourself down.

When speaking assertively, it is useful to phrase your statements beginning with 'I' combined with a clear verb. For example, you might say '*I want...*' or '*I need...*' or '*I feel...*'. It's also helpful, when you wish to be genuinely assertive, to actively seek to understand the other person's perspective, and what they want, need or feel.

One technique when you wish to speak with basic assertiveness is known as the broken record. In the days when people listened to music on black vinyl records, there was sometimes a flaw on the disc which meant that the same snatch of music was repeated and repeated — it was a broken record. Stating and repeating the same phrase can be a powerful way of making a point or a request. As an illustration, let's suppose that you want to return an unsuitable item to a shop. Faced with an unhelpful shop assistant, each time they try to reject your request you might simply repeat the phrase: '*I would like a refund.*' It doesn't always work, but it can be very difficult for the other person to resist.

Assertive people take space – literally and metaphorically – to deliver their message. If you watch someone like Barack Obama giving a speech you will notice that he often speaks very slowly, taking lots of time and space to give his message. It is important to take your time to speak in a confident, clear voice.

Tone of voice and body language are important here. Speaking loudly and aggressively, on the one hand, or meekly and passively, on the other hand, can be unproductive.

As a line manager, you might draw upon some of these ideas to help one of your team to speak and behave more assertively – and perhaps also more confidently. One thing I've noticed is that when someone who has behaved passively for many years begins to behave more assertively, they may feel that they are being aggressive. It can also surprise other people around them who may have benefited from that person's lack of assertiveness in the past.

> **VIDEO**
>
> Assertiveness Training: How to Be Assertive (Lewis Psychology, 2021): www.youtube.com/watch?v=ZeSvcpl2qqU
>
> In this four-minute video Teresa Lewis offers these six tips to improve your assertive communication.
>
> 1. Get in touch with your thoughts, feelings and needs.
> 2. Focus on the problem not the person.
> 3. Keep calm and respectful.
>
> →

4. What do you want?
5. Use 'I' statements.
6. Don't wait.

Reference

Eggert, M (2011) *The Assertiveness Pocketbook*. Winchester: Management Pocketbooks.

INDEX

360-degree feedback, 250

ABCDE model, 262
ABM Amro, 180
action-centred leadership, 228–32
Acton, Lord, 47
Adair, John, 228, 232
Adaptive Leadership, 40–4
Albon, Sarah, 155
AlliedSignal, 174
American Psychiatric Association, 192
American Psychological Association, 190
Ancelotti, Carlo, 186
Aristotle, 27, 114
Ashkenas, Ron, 22
assertiveness, 72, 130, 271–6
authenticity, 5–8, 245
    authentic leadership, 7–8

baby boomer generation, 150
Badaracco, Joseph, 185

Baddeley, Simon, 141
Balogun, Julia, 213
Banks, Bernard, 49
Baskin, Kara, 163
Baxter, Jacqueline, 189
BBC, 162
Ben & Jerry's, 162
Berne, Eric, 9, 242
Blake, Robert, 91, 228
Blakeley, Chris, 61
Blakeley, Karen, 61
Blanchard, Ken, 100
Boisot, Max, 224
Bossidy, Larry, 174
Branson, Richard, 185
Bridges, William, 211–13
Briggs, Katherine, 50
British Association for Counselling and Psychotherapy, 156
British Gas, 161, 176
Brown, Brene, 62
Buehner, Carl, 24

277

Cable, Dan, 238
Cain, Susan, 187, 188, 189
Chaleff, Ira, 181
change, 210–16
Chartered Institute of Marketing, 268
Chartered Institute of Personnel and Development, 85, 134, 175, 201
Christensen, Clayton, 145–9, 166
Clayton, Mike, 80, 105
coaching, 14–18, 37, 93, 99, 122, 174, 220, 235, 240, 264
cognitive behavioural approach, 262–4
Collins, Jim, 187, 237
command and control, 92, 121
confidence, 262–7
conflict, 128–30
consequentialism, 112–13
conversations, 30–4, 66
Cooks-Campbell, Allaya, 117
Coverdale systematic approach, 225–7
Covey, Stephen, 65, 70
Coward, Noel, 116
Cox, Barbara, 52
Cripps, Karen, 64
Critical Issues in Management, 269
Csikszentmihalyi, Mihaly, 191

Dame, John, 239
decision-making, 256–60
delegation, 19–21
Deligiannis, Nick, 135
deontology, 113
development cycle, 265
development reviews, 172, *see* performance and development reviews
Downey, Myles, 233
drama triangle, 243
drivers, 13
Drucker, Peter, 257

East London, University of, 190
Eatough, Erin, 73
Eggert, Max, 273
ego states, 9–12, 93–4, 181, 243, 264
Eisenhower, Dwight, 70
Elkington, John, 109
emails, 252–5
emotional intelligence, 24–9
environmental, social and governance objectives, 108
Epictetus, 262
ethics, 112–15
extraverts, 186–8

Fayol, Henri, 121
feedback, 247–51

finance, 268
Fisher, Roger, 126
followership, 181–3
Ford, Jeffrey, 215
Ford, Laurie, 215
four-player model, 68
French, John, 47
Friedman, Milton, 109

Gallwey, Tim, 233
games, 242–5
Gates, Bill, 185, 236
Gavin, Matt, 7, 8
Gedmin, Jeffrey, 239
Generation X, 151, 153
Generation Y, 151–2, 153
Generation Z, 152–3
George, Bill, 7, 8
Gerras, Stephen, 183
Girdler, Adriana, 255
Goldman Sachs, 176
Goleman, Daniel, 25, 26, 28, 29
Goodwin, Fred, 180
Google, 161, 165
Grant, Adam, 187
Grashow, Alexander, 40
Gratton, Lynda, 132
Greenleaf, Robert, 96, 98
Grint, Keith, 42

Hardingham, Alison, 263
Hart, Jim, 176
Harvard Business School, 187, 216
Health and Safety Executive, 155
Heifetz, Ron, 40, 43, 210
Hofstede, Geert, 204–6
humility, 145–9, 237–42
Hutchinson, Paul, 142
hybrid working, 131–5, 254

Ibarra, Herminia, 18
IBM, 204
ICI, 225, 227
IKEA, 161
impostor syndrome, 235
influencing, 45–7
information, 224–5
inner game, 233–6
introverts, 186–8
I-RIGHT framework, 114–15
Isaacs, Bill, 219

James, Kim, 141
Jaworski, Joe, 97
Johnson, Boris, 237
Jung, Carl, 50

Kant, Immanuel, 113
Kantor, David, 68, 258

Kantor's three languages, 258
Karpman, Stephen, 243
Katzenbach, Jon, 101, 105
Kennedy, Gavin, 143
Kilmann, Ralph, 129
King, Martin Luther, 62, 64
Kolb, David, 36, 39, 222, 225, 227
Kotter, John, 55, 57, 58, 60, 210, 266

leadership, 55–60
LeadershipPlus, 5, 6, 107, 145, 267
leading with love, 61–4
learning from experience, 35–9, 265
Leipzig, Adam, 149
Lewis, Teresa, 246, 275
life positions, 246
Linsky, Marty, 40
listening, 32, 98, 217–21
Lorsch, Jay, 124
Lucidchart, 256
Lupu, Iona, 117

Mackintosh, Joe, 200
management, 55, 56–8, 121, 139, 140, 157–9, 178, 213, 235, 245, 247, 256, 262, 267–70, 275

managerial grid, 91
managing change, 210–16
Mandela, Nelson, 97
marketing, 268
Marsh, Nigel, 120
Maslow, Abraham, 123
Mayer, John, 24
McCall, Morgan, 36, 173
McCombs School of Business, 115
McGregor, Douglas, 122
McKinsey, 210
mediation, 131
meetings, 65–9
Meindl, James, 180
mental health, 133–5, *see also* well-being
mentoring, 17–18, 37, 174
metaphors, 75–80, 94, 139, 140, 161, 218, 222, 232
Meyer, Erin, 206–8, 209
micromanagement, 21–3
MIND, 156
mindfulness, 234
Moore, Martin, 257
Morgan, Gareth, 75, 139, 222
Morse, John, 124
Moulson, Harry, 176, 178, 199
Mouton, Jane, 91, 228

Musk, Elon, 185, 237
Myers, Isabel Briggs, 50
Myers–Briggs Type Indicator, 50–4, 186, 260

Napper, Rosemary, 245
National Careers Service, 140
national culture, 204–9
National Health Service, 156
negotiations, 143, *see also* principled negotiation
Newton, Trudi, 245
Nike, 161

Obama, Barack, 275
Olsen, Erica, 170
organisational culture, 197–203
organisational learning, 222–7
Oxfam, 161, 162

Pentad, 109
performance and development reviews, 36–9, 81–5
PERMA, 191–2
PESTLE framework, 167–9, 170
Peterson, Christopher, 192
Pfeffer, Jeffrey, 159
playing back, 33, 88–9
politics in organisations, 141–3, 144

Polman, Paul, 108, 111
Positive Psychology, 190–6
Positive Psychology Interventions, 194–5
power, 47–9, 62
Praxis, 141
principled negotiation, 126–8, 130
Prospects, 139
Protter, Miles, 179
purpose, *see* values
Putin, Vladimir, 185

questioning, 32, 86–8, 89, 249
quiet leadership, 185–9

Raven, Bertram, 47
Reagan, Ronald, 109
reframing, 263
resistance to change, 215
rights and responsibilities, 272
Riley, Geoff, 260
Rock, David, 186, 210
romance of leadership, 180–1, 183
Royal Bank of Scotland, 180
Ruiz-Castro, Mayra, 117

Salovey, Peter, 24
Sandford, Carol, 109

satisficing, 258, 260
SCARF model, 210
Schaefer, Mary, 95
Schein, Edgar, 198, 202, 240
Schein, Peter, 240
Schrader, Jessica, 190
Scott, Susan, 30, 34, 220
Scoular, Anne, 18
Seligman, Martin, 190, 192, 195
Senge, Peter, 97
Senn Delaney, 176, 177, 200
Senn, Larry, 176
servant leadership, 96–100, 238
shadow of the leader, 176–9
Silbiger, Steven, 270
silence, 219
Simon, Herbert, 258
Smith, Douglas, 101, 105
solution-focused approach, 264
Spears, Larry, 97, 99
Steare, Roger, 114
Stralser, Steven, 270
strategy, 163–4, 268
strengths, 192–3
Su, Jeff, 255
Sustainable Development Goals, 107–8
SWOT analysis, 169–70

talent management, 159–175
Taylor, Bill, 238
Taylor, Mark, 267
teams, 101–6, 229
Thatcher, Margaret, 109, 185
Theory X, 121–5
Theory Y, 121–5
Thomas, Kenneth, 128
Thomas–Kilmann conflict handling model, 129, 272
time management, 70–4
Tomlinson, Ian, 243
Transactional Analysis, 9–13, 242–6
Transco, 101, 102, 176, 178, 199, 200, 259
Treacy, Declan, 252
triple bottom line, 109
Trump, Donald, 185, 237
trust, 234
Tuckman, Bruce, 104
Tyson, Mike, 268

Unilever, 108
United Nations, 107
Ury, William, 126
utilitarianism, 112

values, 145–9
Values in Action Inventory of Strengths, 192
virtue ethics, 113–14
vision, 161–3
voicing, 33, 271
von Moltke, Helmuth, 268
VUCA world, 166–7

Warwick Business School, viii, 1, 5, 42, 103, 107, 112, 114, 131, 145, 153, 204, 267, 269
Warwick, University of, 1, 75, 157, 254, 259
Watkins, Michael, 197

well-being, 155–60
Westergren, Tim, 240
Wheatley, Margaret, 97, 99, 220
Whitaker, David, 102
Whitmore, John, 104, 105, 233
wicked, tame and critical problems, 42–3
Wilson, Jennifer, 153
winner's triangle, 244
Wong, Leonard, 183
work–life balance, 116–20

Young, Jake, 201

zookeeper, 139–40